First World War
and Army of Occupation
War Diary
France, Belgium and Germany

16 DIVISION
49 Infantry Brigade
Royal Irish Regiment
7th Battalion
1 September 1917 - 31 May 1918

WO95/1979/2

The Naval & Military Press Ltd
www.nmarchive.com
Published in association with The National Archives

Published by

The Naval & Military Press Ltd

Unit 10 Ridgewood Industrial Park,

Uckfield, East Sussex,

TN22 5QE England

Tel: +44 (0) 1825 749494

www.naval-military-press.com

www.nmarchive.com

This diary has been reprinted in facsimile from the original. Any imperfections are inevitably reproduced and the quality may fall short of modern type and cartographic standards.

© **Crown Copyright**
Images reproduced by permission of The National Archives, London, England, 2015.

Contents

Document type	Place/Title	Date From	Date To
Heading	1979/2 7 Battalion Royal Irish Regiment Sept 1917-May 1918		
Heading	16th Division 49th Infy Bde 7th Bn Royal Irish Regt Sep 1917-May 1918 To 30 Div 21 Bde Box 2330 Sec 30 Division. 21 Bde Box 2330		
Miscellaneous	Wilds Woodhouse.		
War Diary	Beaurainville	01/09/1917	30/09/1917
War Diary	Maresquel.	03/09/1917	14/10/1917
War Diary	Ervillers	15/10/1917	22/10/1917
War Diary	Left Support. Trenches Div.	23/10/1917	31/10/1917
Miscellaneous	Copy Of Battalion Orders By Major H.E. Norton, South Irish Horse 21st October 1917. App (1)	21/10/1917	21/10/1917
Miscellaneous	Copy Of Battalion Order By Lieut. Colonel C.M. Truman, D.S.O. 27th Oct. 17	27/10/1917	27/10/1917
Miscellaneous	Copy Of Battalion Order By Lieut. Colonel C.M. Truman, D.S.O. Dated 31st October 1917. App (2)	31/10/1917	31/10/1917
War Diary		01/11/1917	30/11/1917
Operation(al) Order(s)	49th Inf. Bde. Order No. 174	30/10/1917	30/10/1917
Miscellaneous	Movement Table To Accompany 49th Inf. Bde. Order No. 174		
Miscellaneous	49th Inf. Bde. Order No. 177	10/11/1917	10/11/1917
Operation(al) Order(s)	Relief Table To Accompany 49th Inf. Bde. Order No. 177		
Diagram etc	Parts of U1 & U7 Fontaine Sheet 51b S.W.		
Miscellaneous	State Of Wire Report.		
Miscellaneous	49th Inf. Bde. No. B.O. 102/1-24-11-17	24/11/1917	24/11/1917
Miscellaneous	49th Inf. Bde. Order No. 182. 24th Nov. 1917	24/11/1917	24/11/1917
Operation(al) Order(s)	49th Inf. Bde. Order No. 183	28/11/1917	28/11/1917
Miscellaneous	Relief Table To Accompany 49th Inf. Bde. Order No. 183		
War Diary	In The Field	01/12/1917	31/12/1917
Operation(al) Order(s)	49th Inf. Bde. Order No. 186	01/12/1917	01/12/1917
Operation(al) Order(s)	Movement Table To Accompany 49th Inf. Bde. Order No. 186		
Operation(al) Order(s)	49th Inf. Bde. Order No. 187	02/12/1917	02/12/1917
Operation(al) Order(s)	49th Inf. Bde. Order No. 189	04/12/1917	04/12/1917
Miscellaneous	March Table To Accompany Brigade Order No 189		
Operation(al) Order(s)	49th Inf. Bde. Order No. 190	05/12/1917	05/12/1917
Miscellaneous	Table To Accompany 49th Inf. Bde. Order No. 190		
Operation(al) Order(s)	49th Inf. Bde. Order No. 192	07/12/1917	07/12/1917
Operation(al) Order(s)	49th Inf. Bde. Order No. 197	11/12/1917	11/12/1917
Operation(al) Order(s)	49th Inf. Bde. Order No. 199	16/12/1917	16/12/1917
Miscellaneous	Move Table To Accompany 49th Inf. Bde. Order No. 199		
Operation(al) Order(s)	49th Inf. Bde. Order No. 200	20/12/1917	20/12/1917
Miscellaneous	Relief Table To Accompany 49th Inf. Bde. Order No. 200		
Operation(al) Order(s)	49th Inf. Bde. Order No. 201	27/12/1917	27/12/1917
Heading	War Diary. For Month Of January, 1918. Volume 47th (S.I.H) R. Irish Regiment.		

War Diary	Ronssoy	01/01/1918	15/01/1918
War Diary	In The Field	16/01/1918	31/01/1918
Operation(al) Order(s)	Operation Order No. 52 by Lt. Col. H.E. Norton Comdg. South Irish Horse (7th R.I. Rgt.) 9th January 1918	09/01/1918	09/01/1918
Operation(al) Order(s)	Operation Order No. 53 by Lt. Col. H.E. Norton Comdg. South Irish Horse (7th R.I. Rgt.) 9th January 1918	15/01/1918	15/01/1918
Miscellaneous	Operation Order No. 54 by Lt. Col. H.E. Norton Comdg. South Irish Horse (7th R.I. Rgt.) 9th January 1918	21/01/1918	21/01/1918
Operation(al) Order(s)	Operation Order No. 55 by Lt. Col. H.E. Norton Comdg. South Irish Horse (7th R.I. Rgt.) 9th January 1918	27/01/1918	27/01/1918
Miscellaneous			
Heading	Vol 5 War Diary For Month of February, 1918. Volume 5 7th (S.I.H) Btn. R Irish Regt.		
War Diary	Lempire	01/02/1918	03/02/1918
War Diary	Hamel	04/02/1918	04/02/1918
War Diary	Villers Faucon	10/02/1918	14/02/1918
War Diary	Epehy Left Sect	15/02/1918	17/02/1918
War Diary	Left Sect	18/02/1918	22/02/1918
War Diary	Epehy	23/02/1918	26/02/1918
War Diary	Right Sub Sect	27/02/1918	28/02/1918
Operation(al) Order(s)	Operation Order No. 62 By Lieut-Col. H.E. Norton, Commanding South Irish Horse, 7th. R. Irish Regt. 28-2-18	28/02/1918	28/02/1918
Operation(al) Order(s)	Operation Order No. 61 By Lieut-Col. H.E. Norton, Commanding South Irish Horse (7th. R. Irish Regt.) 25-2-19	25/02/1918	25/02/1918
Operation(al) Order(s)	Operation Order No 60	21/07/1918	21/07/1918
Operation(al) Order(s)	Operation Order No 59 By Lt-Col H E Norton Commdg South Irish Horse (7th R. Irish) 17th Feby 1918	17/02/1918	17/02/1918
Operation(al) Order(s)	Operation Order No. 58 By Lieut Col H.E. Norton. Commanding South Irish Horse. 7th. R. Irish Regt.	13/02/1918	13/02/1918
Operation(al) Order(s)	Operation Order No. 57 By Lieut Col H.E. Norton. Commanding South Irish Horse 7th. R. Irish Rgt 8th Feby 18	08/02/1918	08/02/1918
Heading	49th Brigade 16th Division. 7th Battalion Royal Irish Regiment March 1918		
War Diary		01/03/1918	05/04/1918
War Diary	Saleux	05/04/1918	05/04/1918
War Diary	Tours-En-Vimeau.	06/04/1918	09/04/1918
War Diary	Woincourt	10/04/1918	10/04/1918
War Diary	Arques	11/04/1918	11/04/1918
War Diary	Campagne	12/04/1918	12/04/1918
War Diary	Wavrans	12/04/1918	14/04/1918
War Diary	Herbelle	15/04/1918	15/04/1918
War Diary	Steenbecque	15/04/1918	19/04/1918
War Diary	Therouanne	20/04/1918	20/04/1918
War Diary	Elnes	20/04/1918	24/04/1918
War Diary	Halinghem	20/05/1918	20/05/1918
War Diary	Therouanne	01/05/1918	01/05/1918
War Diary	Pecquer	01/05/1918	15/05/1918
War Diary	Dohem	16/05/1918	16/05/1918

War Diary	Blenquin	18/05/1918	18/05/1918
War Diary	Samer	19/05/1918	19/05/1918
War Diary	Halinghem	20/05/1918	20/05/1918
War Diary	Frencq	21/05/1918	31/05/1918

1979/2

7 Battalion Royal Irish Regiment

Sept 1917 – May 1918

16TH DIVISION
49TH INFY BDE

7TH BN ROY. IRISH REGT
SEP 1917 - MAY 1918

To 30 DIV 21 BDE
Box 2330

Formed in France out of
South Irish Horse

Box 1974

See 30 DIVISION, 21 BDE,
Box 2330

Miss Woodhouse.

Re attached. According to the War Diaries the South Irish Horse which was a Cavalry Regt went to France in 1915. In August 1917 the Unit was reorganised into an Infantry Battalion and designated 7 (South Irish Horse) Battalion Royal Irish Regt attached to 49 Brigade 16 (Irish) Division. In October 1917 the Battalion Commanding Officer was Lieut Col C.M. TRUMAN DSO and in January 1918 Lieut Col. H E NORTON (See letter 28.1.63). In April 1918 106 Other Ranks all ex cavalry men were posted to Cavalry Base for reposting to Cavalry Units

In June 1918 the Battalion was again reorganised — All Cavalry personnel were transferred to Cavalry for distribution to Cavalry Units and the remaining Infantry personnel together with 835 Irish Reinforcements made up a Battalion designated 7 Battalion Royal Irish Regiment

The War Diaries of 1/1 Northumberland Hussars which are very brief have been examined and there is no record of the Unit having received Reinforcements of any description (This is rather doubtful as the Unit is bound to have received reinforcements to make up for casualties The Diaries just does not record the event)

M Sullivan
26/7/63

NOTE :— I will be glad if you will let me have a copy of your reply as no doubt if the New Zealand ~~Australian~~ people accept the mans service in France he is bound to apply for medals with the result there will be a File in from Army Medal office. I thought he was in France

M.

The above inquiry relates to 73891 Pte Hugh MC CAHON
(correct name MC CHUGHERN)
enlisted 9.2.17 South Irish Horse later as above

Miss Woodhouse
    Re attached
    The South Irish Horse which was a cavalry Regt
went to France

WAR DIARY
INTELLIGENCE SUMMARY
(Erase heading not required.)

7 Bn (S/H) Park Sep '17 to May '18 Vol I

Place	Date	Hour	Summary of Events and Information	Remarks and references to Appendices
BEAURAINVILLE	1-9-17 to 30-9-17		1) Organisation of Battalion and general preparations for Infantry training	
MARESQUEL	3-9-17 to 30-9-17		Surplus Personnel disposed of as under:— Details of Yorkshire Hussars formerly attached 2nd Sh Inch Horse despatched to 33rd Infantry Base Depôt. 4-9-17. Surplus personnel of A.O.C. despatched to A.O.C. Depôt. Calais 5-9-17. Surplus Officers (Unfit) of 2nd South Inch Horse sent to British Cavalry Base Dépôt 5/9/17. Details of Kelo Yeomanry formerly attached 2nd Sh Inch Horse despatched to British Cavalry Base Depôt. 6-9-17. Farriers Shoeing Smiths Saddlers of 1st & 2nd Sh Inch Horse surplus to Battalion despatched to British Cavalry Base Dépôt 7-9-17. Surplus A.V.C. Personnel despatched to A.V.Y. Depôt. Abbeville & A.V.C. Dépôt. Havre. Officers & NCOs attended Courses in Lewis Gunnery, Bombing, Sniping and P.T. Training.	

WAR DIARY
~~INTELLIGENCE SUMMARY~~

(Erase heading not required.)

Army Form C. 2118.

Place	Date	Hour	Summary of Events and Information	Remarks and references to Appendices
MARESQUEL	11-9-16		Officers and NCOs from 16th Division attached to Battalion as instructors	
-do-	30-9-17		Officers and NCOs of Battalion attached to 16th Division in turn for instruction	
			Note:- Also authority received for the designation of the Battalion to be 7th (South Irish Horse) Battalion Royal Irish Regiment.	

J. Rhodes
Major & Adjt
7th (S.I.H.) R. Irish Regt.

4th (S.I. Hostel) Battalion Royal Irish Regiment

WAR DIARY
or
INTELLIGENCE SUMMARY.
(Erase heading not required.)

Army Form C. 2118.

78th DIVISION

Place	Date	Hour	Summary of Events and Information	Remarks and references to Appendices
Marseille	1/10/17		Training as infantry in Lewis Gun, Bombing, Bayonet fighting, Musketry	1 A.B
"	2/10/17		" & Battalion rifle range at HESDIN	2 A.B
"	3/10/17		Lewis Drill Bayonet fighting Physical Training Bombing	3 A.B
"	4/10/17		More advanced platoon drill bayonet fighting + physical training	4 A.B
"	5/10/17		Do as 4/4.	5 A.B
"	6/10/17		Battalion Route March of 9 miles. Draft from EGYPT arrived 2 officers + 60 OR	6 A.B
"	7/10/17		from conducting drawn for MARSEILLES to EGYPT. Inspection of billets.	7 A.B
"	8/10/17		Elementary Company drill. Physical games + controlled charge.	8 A.B
"	9/10/17		Musketry by companies. Lewis Gun + Rifle shooting. Draft from Egypt distribution	7 A.B
"	10/10/17		Company drill + Physical games. Lewis Gun + Musketry	10 A.B
"	11/10/17		Lewis Gun Firing, Bombing Schemes for open warfare attacks	11 A.B
"	12/10/17		Bayonet fighting in assault course. Wiring + trench digging.	12 A.B
"	13/10/17		Advance party 2 officers + 30 OR proceeded BOULEUX to take over camp at ERVILLERS. Physical Training + preparing for move	13 A.B

WAR DIARY
INTELLIGENCE SUMMARY.

Army Form C. 2118.

(Erase heading not required.)

Place	Date	Hour	Summary of Events and Information	Remarks and references to Appendices
Mareuil	14/4/17		Entrained at BEAURAINVILLE and proceeded BOISLEUX au MONT to join 16th Brigade. Took over camp from 7/8th Royal Irish Rifles. (Belfast huts)	2118
ERVILLERS	15/4/17		Company drill and manoeuvre. Saluting & Lewis Gun parade in AM + Rifle & 1 Officer + 50 O.R. to Town Major of ERVILLERS.	2118 
"	16/4/17		Training in Special Attack Platoons. Physical Training, Bombing, Lewis Guns	2118
"	17/4/17		Further training in attack principles. Phys Trg. Bombing, Rifle Bombing, Lewis Guns	2118
"	18/4/17		do. Improvement of camp carried out	2118
"	19/4/17		Battalion inspected by Maj. Gen. Sir R. Hickie C.B. Y.O.C. 16th Division	2118
"	20/4/17		Company drill. Phys. Trg. Improvement of camp continued. Billyarding of Hutments	2118
"	21/4/17		Church parade & talks at ERVILLE R.S.	2118
"	22/4/17		49th Brigade relieved 16th Brigade. 11th Irish Horse arrived and reported in D Coy. Outpost action relieving 2nd Bn. Royal Dublin Fusiliers B Coy in very much distributed at outpost action. One battalion (7/8th Royal Irish Fusiliers) A coming in & Limber R. T17.c.7.6 & Company Strong points C & D Coy. L Company supply details. T17.a.3.2. 1 ration train T7.90 at T. 22.d.8.9.	2118

WAR DIARY
or
INTELLIGENCE SUMMARY.
(Erase heading not required.)

Army Form C. 2118.

Place	Date	Hour	Summary of Events and Information	Remarks and references to Appendices
Left Support Point Hugon	23/10/17		Work on improvements dug-outs re Hugon. Bricked working parties for R.E.	JHS
do	24/10/17		Improvements to dug-outs, wire, re-continued. Company immediate reconstructed new tracking in front line. Working parties under R.E.	JHS
do	25/10/17		Improvements to dug-outs. New dug-out commenced at Bn. H.Qrs. Working parties under R.E.	JHS
do	26/10/17		do	JHS
do	27/10/17		do	JHS
do	28/10/17		South Irish Horse relieved 7th Royal Irish Fusiliers in left sub-section front line. B.Coy. now Left Hugon Coy in Reg Avenue B Company Left centre H.Qrs in Shaft Avenue. A Company Right Centre H.Qrs in Shaft French. S Company Right H.Qrs in Bng Support. Bn Hqrs in Shaft Avenue. Shaft No 122.	JHS
do	29/10/17		Working parties under R.E. Rhy Lane shelled & 2 men killed & 1 wd. A & W Coys Coy emplacements. Enemy trench raided with success by 7th Dnsh Killing Trailers. Three men & two wounded on enemy's retaliatory shell fire, some portions of trenches slightly damaged. Officers patrol went out & reported no wire in front of V.1.5.	JHS
do	30/10/17		Working parties under RE Officers patrol reconnoitred wire in V.14 & V.1.3. Wiring carried out U.1.5	JHS
do	31/10/17		Working parties & improvement of trenches. Much standing re Schwaben Norage. 7HAS furthe all to relief by tomorrow.	JHS

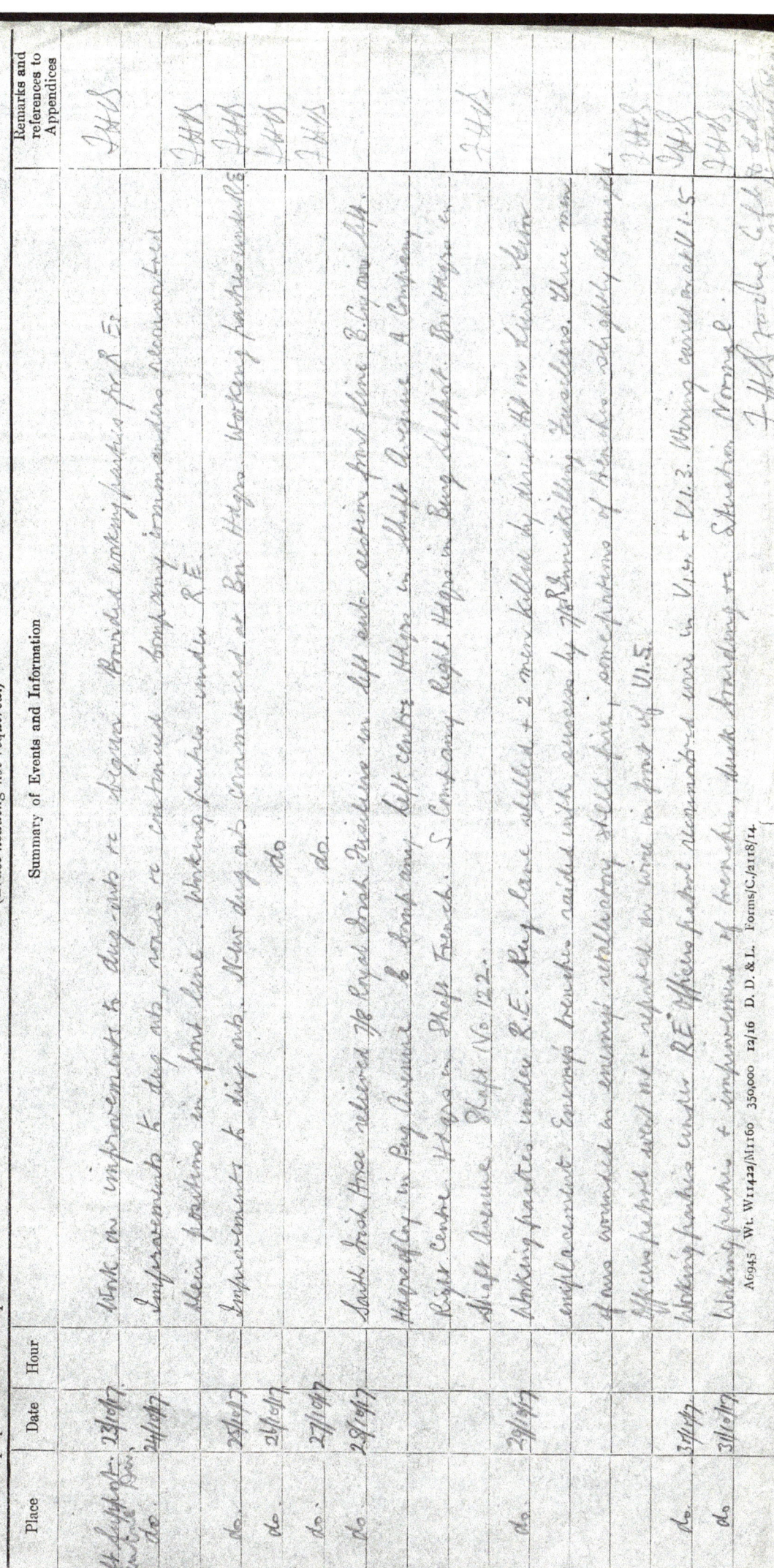

COPY OF BATTALION ORDERS BY MAJOR H.E.NORTON, SOUTH IRISH HORSE

21st October 1917.

1. The 49th Infantry Brigade (less M.G.Coy) will relieve the 48th Infantry Brigade (less M.G.Coy) in the left Section on the 22nd October 1917.

2. The South Irish Horse will relieve the 2nd Royal Dublin Fusiliers in the left Support Sector.

3. Companies will carry out the relief as follows :-

    "A" Company will relieve the Company 2nd Royal Dublin Fus. in the T.17.C.76.

    "B" Company will relieve the Company 2nd Royal Dublin Fusiliers in SHAFT AVENUE (Coy.H.Q.T.6.a.84) Distribution - One platoon HIND TRENCH, three Platoons and Company H.Q. in SHAFT AVENUE. For tactical purposes this Battalion will come under the orders of the O.C.Left front Battalion. On completion of relief the O.C.this Company will report personally to the O.C.Left Front Battalion.

    "C" Company South Irish Horse will relieve the Company 2nd Royal Dublin Fusiliers in strong points C.6. to C.10.(Coy. H.Q. in C.9)

    "S" Company South Irish Horse will relieve the Company 2nd Royal Dublin Fusiliers in SUNKEN ROAD at T.22 a 32. Battalion Headquarters in SUNKEN ROAD at T.22 d 89.

4. Advance parties consisting of an Officer and senior N.C.O. and Gas N.C.O. per Company, Battalion Hd.Qrs and 1 N.C.O per platoon and numbers 1 & 2 of Lewis Gun teams with spare parts will be met by Guides. Further instructions will follow.

ORDERS FOR COMPANIES.

Guides for Companies (1 per Platoon) will be at JUDAS FARM, T.27 c.1(as follows :-
    "B" Coy. 12.15pm) Companies will move off independently
    "C" "   12.45pm) in this order leaving 5 minutes
    "A" "   1.15pm) interval between Platoons. Arrival at
    "S" "   1.45pm) JUDAS FARM must be punctual.

One limber per Company and Headquarters will accompany above carrying rations, ten dixies per Company, filled petrol tins, Mess Box, Officers Packs, Signalling equipment etc. The Quartermaster will issue Periscopes, Very Light Pistols, and these together with wire cutters, wiring gloves and caps will be kept at Company Headquarters.

5. RATIONS AND WATER CART. The daily routine which will commence on 22nd October will be issued later.

6. DRESSING STATION . At Battalion Headquarters,
    hours
7. WORKING IN THE LINE . 9.0am to 12.0noon. 2.0 to 4.0pm.

8. RUNNERS AND CARRYING PARTIES. Will always carry rifles, five rounds in the magazine and at least ten extra rounds.

9. TAKING OVER. Two Runners will report to Battalion Headquarters immediately each Battalion has taken over. Completion of relief will be reported to Battalion Headquarters by the word "SHAMROCK" by 2.45pm.

10. TAKING OVER Blankets, Packs, Kits, will be handed over by Companies to the Quartermaster at Q.M.Store as follows :-

    "B" Coy. 8.15am
    "C" "   8.45am   "S" Coy. 9.45am
    "A" "   9.15am

(2)

11. **PERSONNEL.** The personnel of Officers to go with the Battalion is as under :-

"A" Coy. Capt.Morton, 2/Lieut.Watts, 2/Lieut Stokes, 2/Lieut.Hadden.
"B" Coy. Capt.Furlong, Capt.Colvill, Lieut.Stewart, 2/Lieut. Dwyer.
"C" Coy. Capt.Wardell, Capt.Trant, 2/Lieut Murphy, 2/Lieut. Wilks.
"S" Coy. Capt.Roche Kelly 2/Lieut Barrett, 2/Lieut Harris 2/Lieut Brocklebank.
Hd.Qrs. Commanding Officer, 2nd in Command, Adjutant, Signalling Officer, Intelligence Officer, Medical Officer
2/Lieut Thornley (Lewis Gun Officer) will be attached to "S" Company. 2/Lieut Wolfe Smyth (Bombing Officer will be attached to "B" Company. 2/Lieut Watts will be Works Officer in the Line. He will report to Battalion Headquarters at 3.0pm to-morrow for orders.

12. **INSTRUCTION AND WORK IN THE CAMP.** The following will remain in Transport Lines for duties as detailed. The senior Officer will be in charge and must have a Nominal Roll of all left behind.

BAYONET COURSE.	2/Lieutenants Penhale and Brown.
i/c SIGNALLERS.	2/Lieut. Ferguson.
i/c BUILDING.	2/Lieut Dignan.
PROCEEDING ON LEAVE.	Lieutenants Fogarty, Dease & Smith.
LEWIS GUN INSTRUCTORS.	One N.C.O. from "A" and "B" Companies.
LEWIS GUN CLASS.	Six men per Company.
SIGNALLING CLASS.	The Signalling Officer will arrange for sufficient Signallers to go into the line, the remainder to stay behind for instruction.
BRICKLAYERS.	Two trained, one from "S" and one from "C" Company. Four untrained (for instruction) 1 per Company. Above to report to Building Officer at Orderly Room at 8.45am.
DRYING PARTY.	One man per Company and one from H.Q. will report to senior Officer and will work in the drying room under arrangements to be made by the Quartermaster.

The senior Officer will arrange for instruction in Bombing for all details in addition to their other duties, and will work in conjunction with the building Officer who will get as much work done as possible with the men available.
A nominal Roll will be handed in to the Orderly Room by 7.0pm 21st from Companies and Headquarters of all ranks to be left behind. Also NUMBERS of Trench party.

13. **TENTS** The three tents will be struck and pitched in Transport lines where they will be occupied, until the Battalion moves, by those at present living in them, after which they will be available for details left behind.

14. **IRON RATIONS** Will remain in charge of Quartermaster in Transport lines in bulk.

15. **BROKEN COOKERS.** The Transport Officer will arrange to have these repaired forthwith.

16. **INSPECTION OF CAMP** The Medical Officer will report to the C.O. at 11.30am on 22nd inst that the camp is clean.

(sd) F.H.Brooke, Capt.&Adjt.

Copy of detail of para.5.

1. The Transport Officer will arrange for rations to be delivered until further notice at 4.30pm at :-

    T.17.C.58.   for "A" Company.

    The Duck board
       C.10.   for "B" Company.

    Post C.6.   for "C" Company.

    T.22.A.22   for "S" Company.

    Battb.H.Q.   for Headquarters.

2. WATER. will be delivered as under :-

    "C" Coy.   Post C.6.   at 4.0pm by Water cart.
    "S" "   T.22.a.22.   at 4.30pm ditto
    Batt.H.Q.   T.23.d.27.   at 4.0pm ditto
    "A" Coy.   T.17.c.58.   at 4.30pm ditto
    "B" "   Duck Board C.10. at 4.30pm. X

X This water comes in petrol tins.

3. POST   The post will be sorted at the Transport Lines and sent on limbers to the various Companies,

COPY OF BATTALION ORDERS BY LIEUT/COLONEL C.M.TRUMAN, D.S.O. 27th OCT.17.

1. RELIEF. Battalion will relieve the Battalion holding the left Sector. Companies will relieve in the following order, moving by Platoons at 5 minutes interval :-
LEFT SECTOR "B" "A" "C"

	Move off at.	Relief to be complete by.
"B" Coy.	12.45pm.	1.30pm.
"A" "	1.15pm. (Pass Red Flag)	2.15pm.
"C" "	2.0pm.	3.0pm.

2. RIGHT SECTOR Relief to be complete by 1.45pm

3. LEWIS GUNS Numbers 1 will take over Gun positions one hour before platoons move into the line, Lewis Gun Officer to arrange details.

4. GAS N/C.Os Will move into the line one hour before relief and will render a certificate through the Company Commander to H.Q. that they have personally inspected all gas appliances and that they are in order, or otherwise.

5. POSITION IN LINE

LEFT.	LEFT CENTRE.	RIGHT CENTRE.	RIGHT.
"B"	"C"	"A"	"S"

Code message when relief is complete - "PAT"

6. GUIDES Outgoing Battalion will meet platoons at Red Flag at   and conduct them to their place in the line. The Guides will meet "S" Company at 12.0noon at T.Road, map ref. T.24.a.8.4. sheet 51 B1/20000.

7. ROUTE TO BE TAKEN "A" "B" & "C" via Strong Point at T.10.C.9.9. and Red Flag.
"S" Coy. via CROISELLES to Factory at T.24.a.8.4. Sheet 51.B.1/20000.

8. RATIONS Rations will be dumped as follows :-

H.Qrs. "A" "B" & "C" at STALYBRIDGE at 6.0pm
"S" Company at THE QUARRIES at 4.0pm.

Company Commanders will see that ration carrying parties parade at dump to time.
The Signalling Officer will parade daily at Dump and superintend issue of rations.

9. TRANSPORT Transport of all kinds must never be kept waiting. The Transport Officer has orders to report at once any infringement of this.
C.Q.M.Sergts. when accompanying ration limbers will walk, or ride a mule or bicycle.

10. COOKHOUSES. In future, the Company Cook Corporal will keep a daily strength in a book, showing the strength by Platoons, of men for whom he is cooking - which book will be shown to the C/O. when he goes round.

L/C Mullen will take over the Battalion Cookhouse at STALYBRIDGE on the morning of the 28th inst and remain in charge.

(2)

11. RUNNERS. When in support, Company Runners will act as relay posts and ALL messages will be passed from one Company to another. This arrangement is made to save Runners and expedite messages.
EXAMPLE :-
    Messages from Headquarters to "B" Coy. should go :- From H.Q. to "A" Coy.
          " "A" " "C" "
          " "C" " "B" "

Runners will not carry rifles when taking messages, except in the front line, when they will carry rifle and ten rounds.

12. GUARDS The Commanding Offices does not want Guards to turn out to him unless he tells them to.

13. ROLLS Platoon Leaders, whether Officers or N.C.Os will invariable keep a roll of men under their Command in the trenches, showing how each is employed.

RELIEF ADDENDA The following will proceed to the front line at 12.0noon to take over :-

    1 Officer per Platoon to take over Trench Stores.
    The R.S.M. to take over Bombs etc.
    1182 Sgt.Cook G. "C" Coy. to take over all gas appliances.

RATIONS ADDENDA Dry rations will be taken up in sandbags by Platoons and handed over to Platoon Sergt, by the C.Q.M.S. Wet rations only will go to the Cookhouses.

                                        (sd) A.H.D.Lawson 2/Lt.&A/Adjt.

App(2)

COPY OF BATTALION ORDERS BY LIEUT. COLONEL C.M. TRUMAN, D.S.O.
DATED 31st OCTOBER 1917.

1. **RELIEF :-** The 49th Infantry Brigade will be relieved by the 48th Infantry Brigade in the Left Sector on 1.11.17. The South Irish Horse will be relieved as follows:-
   - "A" Coy. S.I.H. by "D" Coy. 10th R.D.F.
   - "C" "   S.I.H. by "C" Coy. 10th R.D.F.
   - "B" Coy. S.I.H. by "A" Coy. 10th R.D.F.
   - "S" Coy. S.I.H. by "B" Coy. 10th R.D.F.

   Relief to be completed by 4.0pm and to be reported to Battalion Headquarters by the code word "BILL" On relief, S.I.H. will return to BELFAST CAMP.

2. **GUIDES :-** The Signalling Officer will detail two Guides to be at the Red Flag at 11.0am (C.10) to conduct the advance party of the 10th R.D.F. to Headquarters. O.C. "B" "C" & "A" Companies will detail 4 guides each, 1 per Platoon, and the Intelligence Officer 1 Guide for Hd.Qrs. to have a slip of paper on which will be written, his Company and Number of Platoon, to be at the Red Flag at 2.0pm.
   Guides at the Red Flag must not expose themselves until the relief arrives.
   The Companies of the R.D.F. will arrive in the above order, and there must be no delay in the Guides picking up their parties.

3. **ADVANCE PARTY :-** The Advance party consisting of 1 N.C.O. per platoon, 1 N.C.O. from Signallers and 1 N.C.O. from Headquarters, will, with the 4 C.Q.M.Sergts. report to 2/Lieut Dignan and R.Q.M.S.Barber at the Quartermaster's Store ERVILLERS at 10.10am on the 1st November.
   The advance party who take over from "A" Company will report to Company Headquarters at 11.30am.

4. **HANDING OVER :-** All Trench Maps, Defence schemes, Trench Stores Working parties to be found etc. will be handed over and receipts obtained, copies of receipts to reach Orderly Room by 6.0pm on the 1st November. A full statement of work done and to be done will be handed over to the relieving Companies. Aeroplane Photograph Books will not be handed over.

5. **TRANSPORT :** O.C. "A" "B" & "C" Companies and Medical Officer will arrange to dump all material to go on limbers and Maltese Cart, at post C.10. at 2.15pm leaving a guard of two men at the Company dumps. The three limbers and Maltese cart will come at half hour intervals to collect, and will be loaded in order "A" "B" "C" Companies and M.O. Limber for "S" Company at ROYAL DUMP at 4.0pm.

6. **LINES :-** O.C.Companies will see that their lines are clean before handing over. All petrol tins will be taken back to Camp.

7. **WATER :-** O.C.Companies will arrange to leave as much water as possible for the incoming Regiment.

8. **WORKING PARTIES:-** "A" "B" &"C" O.C.Companies will each detail 5 men to report to the R.S.M. at Battalion H.Q. at 9.0am to-morrow. The daily working parties detailed in para. 3 of last night's orders will be continued up to 12.0noon.

(2)

9. **AMMUNITION, GRENADES ETC.**
Companies will render to Orderly Room not later than 10.0am to-morrow, their daily Grenade and Ammunition return made up to 12.0noon.

10. **TRENCH STORES :-** All No.14 Periscopes and French Periscopes should be returned to Brigade H.Q. by 6.0pm on the 2nd prox. Great care should be taken by Battalions in front line to hand over the small oil lamps in Company and Battalion H.Q. Each Company in front line should have one of these.
They should be included in Trench Store List.

GUIDES (ADDENDA)
O.C. "S" Company will detail 4 guides to be at "S" Company H.Q. at 2.30pm.

(sd) F.H.Brooke, Capt. & Adjt.

WAR DIARY
or
INTELLIGENCE SUMMARY.

(Erase heading not required.)

Army Form C. 2118.

Place	Date	Hour	Summary of Events and Information	Remarks and references to Appendices
1917 Nov.	1		Relieved by 10th R. Dublin Fus. in Left Subsection returned to BELFAST CAMP.	Operation order attached
"	2		General cleaning up — Baths.	
"	3		General Training — Baths.	
"	4		Battn. inspected by G.O.C. 49th Inf. Bde. 2 Officers and 80 men on practice digging.	
"	5		Training in Lewis gun, Bombing, Coy. & platoon in the attack, digging.	
"	6		1 Officer & 50 men on fatigue party at Div. H.Q.	
"	7		ditto	
"	7		Lewis gun training, Bombing, Lectures on Trench Warfare. 1 Officer & 50 men fatigue party at Div. H.Q.	
"	8		Trench to trench attack - Coy. v Battn. Bombing down trench. Bayonet fighting. Lewis gun lectures. Rapid wiring. 1 Off. & 50 O.R. fatigue party at Div. H.Q.	
"	9		Physical training & Bayonet fighting. Company tours. Rapid wiring. Fatigue party of 1 Officer & 5 men at Bri. H.Q. Battn strength of others XXXXXXX 30 officers Others about 640 or Bombing. Lewis gun classes. Marching	
"	10		XXXXXX Baths. Out trenches & marching in take.	

Lt. Col. Commanding
SOUTH IRISH HORSE (7th R. R. REGT.)

Army Form C. 2118.

WAR DIARY
or
INTELLIGENCE SUMMARY.
(Erase heading not required.)

Instructions regarding War Diaries and Intelligence Summaries are contained in F. S. Regs., Part II. and the Staff Manual respectively. Title pages will be prepared in manuscript.

Place	Date	Hour	Summary of Events and Information	Remarks and references to Appendices
1917.				
Nov	10.		Physical training & Bayonet fighting. Musketry. Trench to Trench attack. Live bombing. Rapid wiring. Lewis gun classes. Fatigue party 1 Off. & 50 men at Div. H.Q. Lt. Col. C.M. Turner D.S.O. left the Regt. on transfer to "Lurker".	
"	11		Church Parade.	
"	12		Left BELFAST CAMP and relieved 8/9th R. Dublin Fus. holding left Sector. Position in line:- "B" Coy Left Centre "C" Left Centre "A" Right Centre "S" Right. Battn front:- U.1.a.06. (Rag Lane) to V.7.a.29. (Lump Lane) Situation quiet. Relief completed 3.0 pm. Patrolled wire between U.1.d.45.50 & U.1.d.75.35. & found in good condition. Patrolled SENSEE RIVER bed to U.1.b.&.37. Nothing seen; enemy sniper active	movement onto attached
"	13.		Cleaning up positions. Working parties under R.E. daily (125 men) Cleaning trenches, fixing "A" frames, revetting, repairing O.Ps. building Traverses, draining trenches, repairing & improving Cookhouses, fixing & repairing duck boards, completed Lun Boot store, general improvement of posts, putting out wire etc. Situation quiet	

A. M. Lawder
for LT. COL. COMMANDING
SOUTH IRISH HORSE (7th R. I. RGT.)

Army Form C. 2118.

WAR DIARY
or
INTELLIGENCE SUMMARY.
(Erase heading not required.)

Place	Date	Hour	Summary of Events and Information	Remarks and references to Appendices
Nov. 1917	14		Situation quiet. Hostile machine guns active during night.	
"	15		Position in line changed as follows :- "A" Coy SHAFT TRENCH N. of SENSEE RIVER to junction of SHAFT and HORN trenches (exclusive) "C" Coy - junction of SHAFT and HORN trenches (inclusive) to PUG AVENUE. "B" Coy - SHAFT AVENUE and one Platoon in HIND TRENCH. "S" Coy - N. of SENSEE RIVER U.7.a.5.8 to LUMP LANE (inclusive) Relief completed 4/0 p.m. Situation quiet.	
"	16.		Working parties under R.E. supervision as on 13th inst. Our machine guns active. SENSEE RIVER installed.	
"	17		Working parties under R.E. Supervision. Situation normal.	
"	18.		Position in line changed as follows :- "A" Coy - N side SENSEE RIVER to junction FOP LANE and SHAFT TRENCH. "B" Coy - SHAFT AVENUE & 1 Platoon in HIND AV. "C" Coy - part HORN TRENCH & SHAFT TRENCH to junction FOP LANE also junction HIND SUPPORT & FOP LANE to about 150 yds S of SENSEE RIVER. "S" Coy - Strong points C.6 to C.10. Situation normal. Our machine guns very active during night. Working parties under R.E. ceased at mid-day.	

A.P.P. Lumsden
for LT. COL. COMMANDING
SOUTH IRISH HORSE (7th R. I. REGT.)

WAR DIARY
or
INTELLIGENCE SUMMARY

Army Form C. 2118.

Date 1917	Hour	Summary of Events and Information	Remarks and references to Appendices
Nov. 19		Repairing duck boards, and general repairs to trenches. Situation normal. Our machine guns active during night.	
" 20		At 6/20 a.m. our Artillery and machine guns opened intense bombardment on enemy front line — shortly reported very good. 1 Officer & 40 men each from "B" & "S" Coys went over at zero and dug communication trench connecting up LUMP LANE and TUNNEL TRENCH as shown in Red on Map attached. During the operation a gas cylinder was unearthed and damaged causing the following casualties:— 1 Officer (Lt. H. Brocklehurst) and 22 O.R. Also 4 O.R. sustained shell wounds. "A" and "C" Coys. held front line as shown on map — "B" & "S" in support. The enemy reply was heavy at irregular intervals. Two counter attacks were made in front preceded by trench mortars, he was easily repulsed. Faint attacks without tynes were carried out by us against the RIVER ROAD tunnel and supports, seven germans entered our lines with the SENSEE RIVER into HIND SUPPORT and surrendered — 2 were badly wounded. They belonged to the 470th Regt.	
" 21		Our Artillery machine guns continued heavily bombarding the enemy. Enemy retaliated on our lines shelling HIND SUPPORT. During the day the situation became normal. Patrols were sent out at night to ascertain if concentration of troops was taking place, but no amount of movement was heard from the enemy lines.	
" 22		Lewis guns active. Situation normal. Trenches destroyed by shell fire repaired.	

LT. COL. COMMANDING
SOUTH IRISH HORSE (7th R.I. REGT.)

Army Form C. 2118.

WAR DIARY
or
INTELLIGENCE SUMMARY.
(Erase heading not required.)

Instructions regarding War Diaries and Intelligence Summaries are contained in F. S. Regs., Part II. and the Staff Manual respectively. Title pages will be prepared in manuscript.

Place	Date	Hour	Summary of Events and Information	Remarks and references to Appendices
Nov 1917	22		Wiring done at night. Patrol sent out to ascertain if ROTTEN TRENCH was occupied. This was found to be so, but rather lightly held.	
"	23		Trenches cleaned and repaired where blown in. Lewis guns active. Patrol went out to ascertain if ROTTEN TRENCH was strongly held — single shots fired at intervals — apparently being that it was not strongly held. Enemy artillery active — SHAFT TRENCH and HIND SUPPORT shelled but no damage done. Wiring parties went out at night.	
"	24		Heavy enemy shelling on our Right about 6/30 a.m. Otherwise the day was quiet.	
"	25		Battalion relieved by 7/8th R. Irish Fusiliers and returned to BELFAST CAMP	movement order attached
"	26		Cleaning and checking equipment.	
"	27		Baths	
"	28		Inspection by G.O.C. H.q 16th Inf. Bde.	
"	29		Practised trench to trench attack first by Coys. and then as a Battalion. Free marching order pounds. Certain officers went to reconnoitre the Centre Subsection.	
"	30		Left BELFAST CAMP and took over Centre Subsection from 2nd R. Innis. Fusiliers. 1 Officer (Capt G.C. Colinee) and 5 O.R. killed 2 O.R. missing and 1 O.R. slightly wounded during the relief.	movement order attached

LT. COL. COMMANDING
SOUTH IRISH HORSE (7th R. I. REGT.)

S E C R E T.   Copy No ..6..

49th Inf. Bde. Order No. 174.

30th October 1917.

1. The 49th Inf. Bde. (less M.G.Company) will be relieved in the Left Section by the 48th Inf. Bde. (less M.G.Company) on 1st November in accordance with attached table.

2. All details will be arranged between Unit Commanders concerned.

3. Advance parties, to include Snipers, Observers, Nos. 1 of Lewis Gun Teams and Brigade Bomb Store Keepers will take over 4 hours before their respective reliefs.

4. Billeting parties of 49th Inf. Bde. will report at their respective Camps by 11 a.m. 1st November.

5. All trench stores, defence plans, working party lists, work in progress and proposed, etc, will be carefully handed over and receipts taken. Copies of receipts to be sent to Brigade Headquarters by 6 p.m. 2nd November. Aeroplane photos will not be handed over.

6. Completion of relief will be notified by code word - "ENNISKILLEN".

7. Headquarters, 49th Inf. Bde. will close at T.21.d.4.9 and open at HAMELINCOURT on completion of relief, at which hour command of Left Section will pass from G.O.C. 49th Inf. Bde. to G.O.C. 48th Inf. Bde.

8. ACKNOWLEDGE.

T.D.MacDonald. Captain,
Brigade Major, 49th Infantry Brigade.

Issued through Signals.

Copy No. 1 to G. O. C.
     " 2 Staff Captain.
     " 3 Bde. Signal Officer.
     " 4 Bde. Supply Officer.
     " 5 2nd R. Irish Regt.
     " 6 7th (S.I.H) R. I. Regt.
     " 7 7/8th R. Innis Fus.
     " 8 7/8th R. Irish Fus.
     " 9 49th M.G.Company.
     " 10 49th T.M.Battery.
     " 11 47th Inf. Bde.
     " 12 48th Inf. Bde.
     " 13 152nd Inf. Bde.
     " 14 16th Div. (G).
     " 15 16th Div. (Q).
     " 16 A. D. M. S.
     " 17 180th Bde. R.F.A.
     " 18 174th Coy, A.S.C.
     " 19-20 War Diary.
     " 21 File.

MOVEMENT TABLE TO ACCOMPANY 49TH INF. BDE. ORDER NO. 174.

Unit to be relieved.	Relieving Unit.	Location.	Relief to be complete by:	Relieved unit marches to:
7/8th R. Innis Fus.	2nd R. Dublin Fus.	Right Subsection.	5 p.m.	ENNISKILLEN CAMP.
7th (S.I.R) R.I. Regt.	1st R. Dublin Fus.	Left Subsection.	4 p.m.	BELFAST CAMP.
2nd R. Irish Regt.	1st R. Dublin Fus.	Right Support.	2 p.m.	CLONMEL CAMP.
7/8th R. Irish Fus.	8/9th R. Dublin Fus.	Left Support.	3 p.m.	ARMAGH CAMP.
49th T.M. Battery.	49th T.M. Battery.	Right & Left Subsections.	5 p.m.	Camp vacated by 48th T.M. Battery.

NOTES :- All movement to be by platoons at 5 minutes interval.

Rendezvous for guides should not be in immediate neighbourhood of Forward Brigade H.Q.

		Time	
"A"	20.	8.30 —	Coy Hqrs
"A"	2.		Trench party
"B"	24.	8.30	Coy Hq
B	1		Trench party
C	24.	8.30	Coy Hqrs
C	1.		Trench party
Support	22 (includes ho 10)	8.15	× Fun. Hind
	22 (" no 11)	8.15	× Fast. Hind
S.	10.	9–12 / 2–4	?
S.	16.	10 pm – 2 am	?

S E C R E T.　　　　　　　　　　　　　Copy No ..6...

49th Inf. Bde. Order No. 177.

10th November 1917.

1. (a) The 7/8th R. Innis Fus. and 7th (S.I.H) R. Irish Regt. will take over the Right and Left Subsections of the Left Section respectively on the 12th instant.

   (b) The 2nd R. Irish Regt. and 7/8th R. Irish Fus. will be relieved by two Battalions 48th Inf. Bde. in the Left and Right Support Positions respectively on the 12th instant.
   The reliefs will be carried out according to attached Table.

   (c) The 49th T.M.Battery will relieve the 48th T.M.Battery in the Left Section on 12th instant.

   (d) The 49th Inf. Bde.H.Q. will relieve the 48th Inf. Bde. H.Qrs. in the Left Section on the 13th instant.

2. Details of relief will be arranged between unit commanders concerned.

3. The following will be carefully taken over :-

   (a) All trench stores, maps, defence plans.
   (b) All work in progress and proposed.

   A list of all trench stores and ammunition taken over or handed over will be forwarded to Brigade H.Q. by 6 p.m, 13th instant.

4. Advance parties, including snipers, observers and Nos. 1 of Lewis Gun Teams from units taking over will take over 4 hours before their respective reliefs commence.

5. Completion of relief will be reported to Brigade Headquarters by code word "GAZA".

6. ACKNOWLEDGE.

　　　　　　　　　　　　　　　　　T.L.Macdonald. Captain,

　　　　　　　　　　Brigade Major, 49th Infantry Brigade.

Issued through Signals.

Copy No. 1 to G. O. C.　　　　　11 to 48th Inf. Bde.
　　..　2　　Staff Captain.　　　12　　102nd Inf. Bde.
　　..　3　　Bde. Signal Officer.　13　　16th Division (G).
　　..　4　　Bde. Supply Officer.　14　　16th Division (Q).
　　..　5　　2nd R. Irish Regt.　　15　　A.D.M.S.
　　..　6　　7th (S.I.H) R.I.Rgt.　16　　180th Bde. R.F.A.
　　..　7　　7/8th R. Innis Fus.　　17　　144th Coy, A.S.C.
　　..　8　　7/8th R.Irish Fus.　　18　　155 Field Coy, R.E.
　　..　9　　49th M.G.Company.　　 19　　157 Field Coy, R.E.
　　..　10　 49th T.M.Battery.　　 20-21 War Diary.
　　..　11　 47th Inf. Bde.　　　　22　　File.

RELIEF TABLE TO 30th AND 49th INF. BDE. ORDER NO. 177.

Relieving Unit.	Unit to be relieved.	Location.	Relief to be complete by.	Relieved unit marches to
7/8th R. Innis Fus.	1st R. Dublin Fus.	Right subsection.	3 p.m. 12th instant.	Right Support.
7th (S.H.) R.I.Regt.	8/9th R. Dublin Fus.	Left sub-section.	3 p.m. 12th instant.	Left Support.
1st R. Dublin Fus.	7/8th R. Irish Fus.	Right Support.	5 p.m. 12th instant.	ARMAGH CAMP.
8/9th R.Dublin Fus.	2nd R.Irish Regt.	Left Support.	5 p.m. 12th instant.	ENNISKILLEN CAMP.
48th T.M.Battery.	18th T.M.Battery.	Right and Left Subsections.	5 p.m. 12th instant.	Camp vacated by 10th T.M.Battery.
49th Inf. Bde. H.Q.	29th Inf. Bde. H.Q.	Left Bde. H.Qrs.	4 p.m. 13th instant.	Res. Bde. H.Qrs.

2nd R. Dublin Fus. will move from ARMAGH CAMP to BELFAST CAMP. Move to be complete by 3 p.m.
10th R. Dublin Fus. will remain in CLONMEL CAMP.
Platoons will move at 5 minutes interval.
Guides will met rendezvous in neighbourhood of Forward Brigade Headquarters.
Battalions proceeding to Camps will take over working parties from battalions vacating.
Billeting parties will report at their respective Camps at 11 a.m.

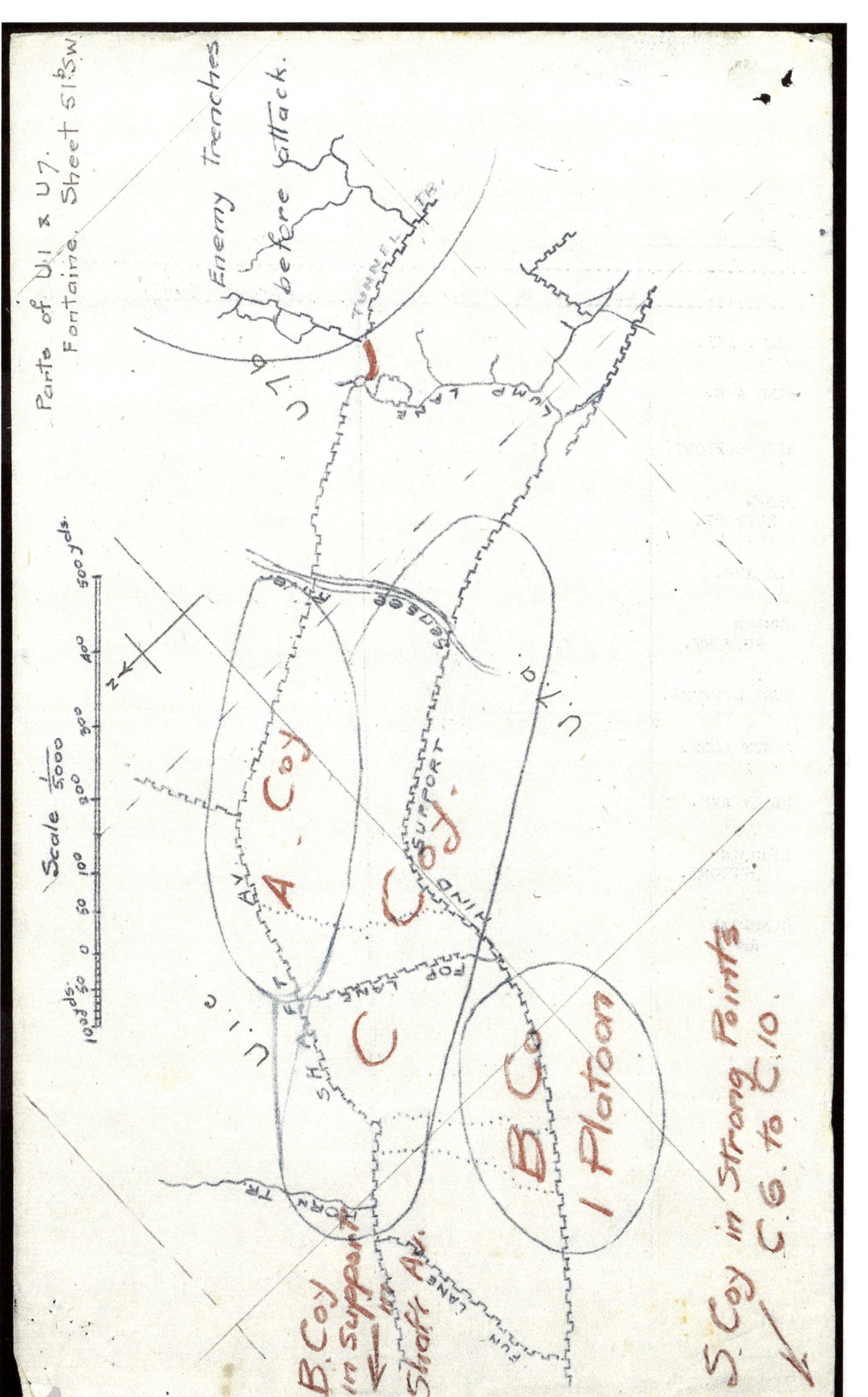

STATE OF WIRE REPORT.

Left Section.

TRENCH.	CONDITION OF WIRE.	NATURE OF WIRING.
SHAFT AVE.		
HIND AVE.		
HIND SUPPORT.		
BROWN SUPPORT.		
PUG AVE.		
HUMBER SUPPORT.		
BURG SUPPORT.		
JANET LANE.		
NELLY AVE.		
LINCOLN SUPPORT.		
GUARDIAN RES.		

S E C R E T.   Copy No ....

All recipients of 49th Inf. Bde.

Order No. 182 of today's date.

49th Inf. Bde. No. B.O. 182/1 - 24-11-17.

The following additional paragraph will be made to 49th Inf. Bde. Order No. 182 :-

The 48th T.M.Battery will relieve the 49th T.M.Battery in the CENTRE and LEFT Subsections tomorrow. Relief to be complete by 4 p.m. 49th T.M.Battery will, on completion of relief, proceed to MOYNE CAMP.

T.C. MacDonald.   Captain,
Brigade Major, 49th Infantry Brigade.

S E C R E T.   Copy No. 6

49th Inf. Bde. Order No. 122.

24th Nov. 1917.

1. The 2nd R. Dublin Fus. and 7/8th R. Irish Fus. will relieve the 7/8th R. Innis Fus. and 7th (S.I.H) R.Irish Regt. in the CENTRE and LEFT SUBSECTIONS respectively tomorrow, 25th instant.

2. Details will be arranged between Commanding Officers concerned.

3. 7/8th R. Innis Fus. will attach two platoons complete to the 2nd R. Irish Regt. from tomorrow. O.C. 7/8th R. Innis Fus. will arrange for them to report to 2nd R. Irish Regt. by 12 noon 25th.

4. (a) All trench stores, No. 9 Periscopes, gun boots, ammunition, grenades, etc, will be carefully handed and taken over. A return of above will be rendered to reach this office by 6 p.m. 26th. Particular attention will be paid to No. 9 Periscopes and gum boots.

(b) All work in hand and proposed will be carefully handed over in writing to ensure continuity.

5. Relief of Left Subsection to be complete by 4 p.m. and Centre Subsection by 5 p.m.

6. Advanced parties to include observers, snipers and Nos. 1 of Lewis Gun Teams, will take over 4 hours before their respective reliefs.

7. On completion of relief 7th (S.I.H) R.I.Regt. will march to BELFAST CAMP, and the 7/8th R. Innis Fus. to ENNISKILLEN CAMP. Billeting parties will take over camp by 11 a.m.. 1st R. Dublin Fus. will march to ARMAGH CAMP.

8. All movements will be made by platoons at 5 minutes interval.
Owing to bad state of MOLE LANE it will not be used for purposes of relief during daylight unless completed tonight.

9. Command of LEFT SECTION will pass to G. O. C. 48th Inf. Bde. on completion of relief.
H.Q. 49th Inf. Bde. will then move to HAMELINCOURT.

10. Completion of relief will be notified to 48th & 49th Inf. Bde. H.Q. by Code Word "VICTORY".

11. ACKNOWLEDGE.

                                    MacDonald Captain,
Brigade Major, 49th Infantry Brigade.

Issued through Signals.

Copy No.				
1	G. O. C.	11	16th Div. (G).
2	Staff Captain,	12	16th Div. (Q).
3	Bde. Signal Officer,	13	16th Div. Artillery.
4	Bde. Int. Officer.	14	180th Bde. R.F.A.
5	2nd R.Irish Regt.	15	47th Inf. Bde.
6	7th (S.I.H) R.I.Regt.	16	48th Inf. Bde.
7	7/8th R. Innis Fus.	17	Left Brigade.
8	7/8th R. Innis Fus.	18	157th Field Coy, R.E.
9	49th M.G.Company.	19	114th Coy, A.S.C.
10	49th T.M.Battery.	20-21	War Diary.
		22	File.

S E C R E T.   Copy No 6.

49th Inf. Bde. Order No. 183.

28th Nov. 1917.

1. The 49th Inf. Bde. will relieve the 48th Inf. Bde. in the Left Section on 30th November according to attached march table.

2. All details will be arranged between Os.C. Units concerned.

3. The Subsections of the LEFT SECTION are as follows :-

    Brigade Headquarters   T.21.d.5.9.

    Right Subsection.   U.14.a.7.2 to U.8.c.1.2.

        Headquarters U.13.b.9.1.

    Centre Subsection.   U.8.c.1.2 to U.7.b.4.2.

        Headquarters U.7.c.9.8.

    Left Subsection.   U.7.a.8.2 to U.1.c.1.8.

        Headquarters T.6.d.40.95.

4. (a) All trench stores, plans of defence, No. 9 Periscopes, ammunition, grenades, etc, will be carefully taken over.

   (b) All work in progress and proposed will be carefully taken over in writing to ensure continuity of work.

   Aeroplane photographs will not be taken over.

   A return of above will be forwarded to Brigade H.Q. by 6 p.m. 1st December.

5. Advance parties, to include snipers, observers and Nos. 1 of Lewis Gun teams, will take over four hours before their respective reliefs.

   Billeting parties will report to their respective camps by 11 a.m. 30th instant.

6. All units will send to Brigade H.Q. a sketch showing their dispositions to include Headquarters, posts and Lewis Guns as soon as possible after taking over.

7. Completion of relief will be notified to Brigade H.Q. by code word "DOVER", when command of Left Section will pass to G.O.C. 49th Inf. Bde.

8. ACKNOWLEDGE.

                                        J.A. MacDonald. Captain,

                                Brigade Major, 49th Infantry Brigade.

Issued through signals.

Copy No.				
1	G.O.C.	12	16th Division (Q).
2	Staff Captain.	13	16th Div. Artillery.
3	Bde. Signal Officer.	14	47th Inf. Bde.
4	Bde. Int. Officer.	15	48th Inf. Bde.
5	2nd R. Irish Regt.	16	Left Brigade.
6	7th (S.I.H) R.I.Regt.	17	180th Bde. R.F.A.
7	7/8th R. Innis Fus.	18	157th Field Coy. R.E.
8	7/8th R. Irish Fus.	19	144th Coy. A.S.C.
9	49th M.G. Company.	20-21	War Diary.
10	49th T.M. Battery.	22	File.
11	16th Division (G).		

RELIEF TABLE TO ACCOMPANY 49th INF. BDE. ORDER No. 183.

Relieving Unit.	Unit to be relieved.	Location.	Relief to be complete by:	Relieved unit marches to:	Remarks.
2nd R.Irish Regt.	8/9th R. Dublin Fus.	Right Subsection.	3 p.m.	ENNISKILLEN CAMP.	2 platoons in QUARRY.
7th (S.I.H) R.I.Rgt.	2nd R. Dublin Fus.	Centre Subsection.	3 p.m.	BELFAST CAMP.	2 platoons in QUARRY.
7/8th R.Innis Fus.	10th R. Dublin Fus.	Support.	3 p.m.	CLONMEL CAMP.	1 Coy.sunken rd.T.23.a. 1 Coy.sunken rd.T.23.c. 1 Coy.sunken rd.T.23.c. 1 Coy.sunken rd.T.23.c.
1st R. Dublin Fus.	7/8th R.Irish Fus.	Left Subsection.	4 p.m.	ARMAGH CAMP.	
49th T.M.Battery.	48th T.M.Battery.	Left Section.	4 p.m.	MOYNE CAMP.	

All movement to be by platoons at 5 minutes interval.

The platoons at QUARRY will be utilised as carrying parties for rations, etc. for their respective Battalions.

WAR DIARY or INTELLIGENCE SUMMARY

Army Form C. 2118.

(Erase heading not required.)

Place	Date	Hour	Summary of Events and Information	Remarks and references to Appendices
The Field	Dec 1917 1		Battle holding Battn Sylvester + Stratton he cond - 2/19 Rs according to order of relief	A/K/L
	2		Relieved by 2/1st Middlesex Regt marched back to Belgian Camp ERVILLERS (both billets muddy)	A/K/L
	3		Battn left ERVILLERS at 10/30am marched to BARASTRE	A/K/L
	4		Standing to to move at ½ hours notice from BARASTRE	A/K/L
	5		Marched to TINCOURT + billeted there for the night (Slung gr. Bde attd)	A/K/L
	6		Battn marched to ST EMILIE (copy of movement order extd)	A/K/L
	7		Reinforcement in support Outpost line in front of ST EMILIE from 5.0am to 2pm.	A/K/L
	-		Battn returned to Billets. Equipped checked. Battn left ST EMILIE + relieved the 1st R. Suff. Fus. on the Left Section (copy of order attd)	A/K/L
	8		Battn on Left Section - Situation normal	A/K/L
	9		Situation normal - Repairing trenches etc - working parties at night	A/K/L
	10		Situation quiet during day - hostile aircraft etc. Enemy heavy bombardment at night about 25 Germans seen by our post W. side of LEMPIRE Rd. succeeded towards PRIEL COTTAGE. About an hours fighting of a party who returned towards CATELET COPSE, was beaten off by our post + Lewis Gun on by our Lewis gun 2 of the Germans were killed + 3 captured (included Officer) Our casualties were 2 of our men were wounded. Most gallant conduct by the NCO i/c was responsible to N.G.S. with + O Blts ranks by Gas from trenches opposed. Enemy artillery active shelling front line from PRIEL FARM to CATELET COPSE (50 shells "P" calibre) Our Machine guns active during night + Rifle in vicinity of EAGLE QUARRY	A/K/L
	11		Went to PRIEL FARM with much more front line from BRIGADE command during the	A/K/L

A/K/Laughton Captain

WAR DIARY
or
INTELLIGENCE SUMMARY.
(Erase heading not required.)

Army Form C. 2118.

Place	Date Dec	Hour	Summary of Events and Information	Remarks and references to Appendices
	12		Battn. relieved in evening by 7/8 R. Scots. Two men attached to HQrs at ST EMILIE killed, shelled v. 2.8 men killed & 4 wounded. Lewis gunner & 1 O.R. wounded during relief. Battn. moved out of billets & occupied Railway Cutting	copy moved into AWD A.W.D.
	13		2 Coys. had baths at Villers Faucon. Battn. mainly occupied cleaning up & erecting huorance etc in Railway Cutting	A.W.D.
	14		Remaining 2 Coys had baths at Villers Faucon. A working party of 4 officers and 170 O.R.s were supplied to make XX to forward area.	A.W.D.
	15		Improving shelters during morning. In afternoon a working party of 4 offrs and 250 men were supplied to work in forward area under Staff Pioneers	A.W.D.
	16		Enemy art. checked - Small working party supplied to Town Major, R.E. district heavily shelled at night. 1 man wounded.	A.W.D.
	17		Battn relieved by 8/9 R. Innis. Fus. and marched to BUISE and occupied billets vacated by the 2nd R. Irish Fus. Heavy fall of snow (copy order attd.)	A.W.D.
	18		Battalion rested	A.W.D.
	19		Battn. marched to TINCOURT relieving 1st VILLIERS FAUCON & occupied billets vacated by Leicesters	A.W.D.
	20		Battle for half of Battn. Lewis gun class resumed	A.W.D.
	21		Baths for remainder of Battn.	A.W.D.
	22		Parade by Coys for inspection & checking of equipment. Left Section of the Right Sector reconnoitered by a party.	A.W.D.
	23		Church Parades. Relieved 6th Conn. Rangers in the Left Section of the Right Sector. Heavy shelling of LEMPIRE VILLAGE during night. (copy of movement order attd)	A.W.D.

Capt. ????

WAR DIARY
or
INTELLIGENCE SUMMARY

Army Form C.2118.

Place	Date Dec	Hour	Summary of Events and Information	Remarks and references to Appendices
	24		Very quiet. Intermittent shelling from 6.0 p.m. many shells the usual round Batln HQ between 7 & 8 p.m.	AA&L
	25		Heavy shelling of village of LEMPIRE all round Batln HQ at 10 am. Day was quiet.	AA&L
	26		Several aircraft dropped 4 bombs on TOMBOIS FARM at 9.10 am - no damage done. Shop in front line were intermittently shelled - no casualties. One man wounded by a stray bullet.	AA&L
	27		A quiet day - more snow fell & visibility bad.	AA&L
	28		Visibility good. Enemy aircraft active. Otherwise a quiet day. Intermittent shelling during night.	AA&L
	29		Enemy aircraft active. Otherwise a quiet day. Batln were relieved by 7 B.R. Regt & marched to Southrust Huts via RONSSOY taking over billets occupied by 7/8 Innis Fus. (Catering movement under ests)	AA&L
	30		A very quiet day with visibility bad. Small working parties supplied to R.E.	AA&L
	31		A quiet day. Working parties of 1 Officer and 45 other ranks per Coy were supplied to R.E. for work on RONSSOY defence.	AA&L

A.W. Lawson
Capt + Adjt

S E C R E T.   Copy No ..4

49th Inf. Bde. Order No. 186.

1st December 1917.

1. The 16th Division (less Artillery, Field Coys. R.E. and Pioneers) is being relieved in the line at once by 40th Division, (less Artillery, Field Coys R.E. and Pioneers).

2. The 49th Inf. Bde. (with 1st R. Dublin Fus. but less 7/8th R. Irish Fus) will be relieved in the LEFT SECTION by the 121st Inf. Bde. on December 2nd and night of 2nd/3rd in accordance with attached table.

3. Advance parties, to include snipers, observers, Nos. 1 of Lewis Gun Teams and Brigade Bomb Store keepers will take over during the morning of 2nd December.

4. Billeting parties of 49th Inf. Bde. will report at respective camps by 11 a.m. 2nd December.

5. All trench maps of 1/10,000 and 1/20,000 scale, air photographs, trench stores, plans for future work, defence plans, working party lists, etc, will be carefully handed over and receipts taken. Copies of receipts to be sent to Brigade H.Q. by noon 3rd December. No. 9 periscopes and No. 18 (Vigilant) periscopes will be brought out of the line, and NOT handed over.

6. No troops are to be withdrawn until they have been properly relieved.

7. Completion of relief will be wired to Brigade H.Q. by code words as follows :-

    Right Subsection.   CAVALRY.
    Centre Subsection.   GUNNER.
    Left Subsection.   INFANTRY.
    Support Battalion.   SAPPER.
    M.G. Company.   CYCLIST.
    T.M. Battery.   MEDICAL.

8. On and West of the main BAPAUME-ARRAS Road intervals of 200 yards will be maintained between Battalions, Battalion Transport and similar units. Attention is drawn to the Instructions as to March Discipline issued under 49th Inf. Bde. No. S.G.C. 12/121 dated 9.11.17.

9. (a) Two platoons of R. Innis Fus. attached to 2nd R. Irish Regt. will return to their own unit on completion of relief.

    (b) All personnel attached to 157th Field Coy, R.E. have been ordered to rejoin their own units.

10. Headquarters, 49th Inf. Bde. will close at T.21.d.4.9 and open at HAMELINCOURT on completion of relief, at which hour command of LEFT SECTION will pass from G.O.C. 49th Inf. Bde. to G.O.C. 121st Inf. Bde.

11. ACKNOWLEDGE.

Captain,

A/Brigade Major, 49th Infantry Brigade.

Issued through Signals at .... p.m.

```
Copy No.  1 to  G. O. C.
     "    2      Staff Captain.
     "    3      2nd R. Irish Regt.
     "    4      7th (S.I.H) R.I. Regt.
     "    5      7/8th R. Innis Fus.
     "    6      1st R. Dublin Fus.
     "    7      49th M.G. Company.
     "    8      49th T.M. Battery.
     "    9      Bde. Signal Officer.
     "   10      Bde. Int. Officer.
     "   11      Bde. Transport Officer.
     "   12      47th Inf. Bde.
     "   13      103rd Inf. Bde. (for inf).
     "   14      16th Division (G).
     "   15      16th Division (Q).
     "   16      16th Div. Artillery.
     "   17      A. D. M. S.
     "   18      180th Bde. R.F.A.
     "   19      121st Inf. Bde.
     "   20      155th Field Coy, R.E.
     "   21      157th Field Coy, R.E.
     "   22      144th Coy, A.S.C.
     "   23-24   War Diary.
     "   25      File.
```

MOVEMENT TABLE TO ACCOMPANY 49th INF. BDE. ORDER No. 186.

Unit to be relieved.	Relieving Unit.	Location.	Guides.	Remarks.	Relieved unit moves to :
2nd R. Irish. Regt.	12th Suffolk Regt.	RIGHT SUBSECTION.	As arranged by C.O's of units.	Details of relief to be arranged by unit Commanders concerned.	CLONMEL CAMP.
7th (S.I.H) R.I.Rgt.	21st Middlesex Rgt.	CENTRE SUBSECTION.	As arranged by C.O's of units.		BELFAST CAMP.
1st R. Dublin Fus.	20th Middlesex Rgt.	LEFT SUBSECTION.	See (a) below.		ARMAGH CAMP.
7/8th R. Innis Fus.	13th York. Regt.	SUPPORT.	See (b) below.		ENNISKILLEN CAMP.
49th M.G.Company.	121st M.G.Company.	Right, Centre and Left Subsections	To be arranged between unit commanders concerned.		MOYNE CAMP.
49th T.M.Battery.	121st T.M.Battery.	Right and centre subsections.			MOYNE CAMP.

(a) 1st R. Dublin Fus. will provide one guide per platoon, 1 per Coy. H.Q. 1 per Battalion H.Q. all under an officer who will meet relieving unit at MAISON ROUGE T.35.c.8.9 at time to be wired later.

(b) 7/8th R. Innis Fus. will provide same party as in (a) to be at MAISON ROUGE at time to be wired later.

Movement to be by platoons at 500 yards distance.

SECRET.   Copy No 4.

48th Inf. Bde. Order No. 187.

Reference Map Sheet 57.c.   2nd December 1917.
1/40,000.

1. (a). The 16th Division (less Artillery, Field Coys, R.E, and Pioneers) will move tomorrow, December 3rd, to the area ROCQUIGNY - BARASTRE - BEAULENCOURT.

   (b). The 48th Inf. Bde (less 7/8th R.Irish Fus. but with 1st R. Dublin Fus), and with 113th Field Ambulance and 144th Coy. A.S.C. will move to BARASTRE Area tomorrow, 3rd December 1917 according to attached March Table.

2. **Dinners** will be cooked in cookers on route, and will be served out on arrival at destinations.

3. **Billeting Parties** as follows will report to Staff Captain at Town Major's Office, BARASTRE, at 10 a.m. 3rd December 1917 :-

   Battalions (including 7/8th R.Irish Fus.but <u>excluding</u> 1st R. Dublin Fus.) each - 1 Officer 5 Other Ranks on horses or cycles.
   M.G.Company - 1 Officer 2 Other Ranks, on horses or cycles.
   T.M.Battery - 1 N.C.O on cycle.
   Bde. H.Q. - Sgt Johnston on a cycle.
   Interpreters - M. Laguerre and M. Keisel - (Lieut. Quinn will warn former, 2nd R. Irish Regt. will warn latter).

   Each unit's party and the two interpreters must be in possession of map sheet 57.c. scale 1/40,000, and each unit's party must know exact billeting strength in officers, O.R., horses and vehicles.

4. **Supply Wagons** of units will march with 144th Coy. A.S.C. 1 representative from units concerned will be sent by Staff Captain from BARASTRE to cross roads C.2.b.0.8 to act as guides for these wagons to unit's camps.

5. All **Trained Reinforcements** from Depot Battalion will join Brigade Headquarters tomorrow as it passes through SAPIGNIES. These reinforcements will be sent to Battalions as soon as guides from battalions reach new Brigade H.Q.

6. **Rear Parties** under an officer will be left behind to clean and hand over camps and transport lines to units of 120th Inf. Bde.

   Each party will obtain receipts and usual certificates as to cleanliness from incoming units, and will rejoin their units as soon as possible afterwards.

7. **Motor Lorries** for 1st blankets have been allotted as follows :-

   One to each Battalion.
   One to M.G.Company and T.M.Battery.
   One to Brigade Headquarters.
   These will be at present camps at 8 a.m.
   In case of each <u>Battalion only</u> - its motor lorry may be sent back on a second journey to Boxing Hall, ERVILLERS, (or camp as case may be) to bring to new destination the <u>second blankets.</u>

   A suitable guards must accompany each load, and an intelligent guide with a map must be on the lorry. These guides will learn their new destinations on applying to Staff Captain at Town Major's Office, BARASTRE.

8.   Distances as follows will be observed on the march :-

   200 yards between Companies.
   200 yards between battalions.
   200 yards between each Battalion and its transport.

9.   ACKNOWLEDGE.

                                        Captain,

            A/Brigade Major, 49th Infantry Brigade.

Issued through Signals at 11.45 p.m.

        Copy No. 1 to G. O. C.
        "   2   Staff Captain.
        "   3   2nd R.Irish Regt.
        "   4   7th (S.I.H) R.I.Regt.
        "   5   7/8th R. Innis Fus.
        "   6   1st R. Dublin Fus.
        "   7   7/8th R.Irish Fus.(through
                                    48th.Bde.)
        "   8   49th L.G.Company.
        "   9   49th T.M.Battery.
        "   10   48th Inf. Bde.
        "   11   114th Coy, A.S.C.
        "   12   115th Field Ambulance.
        "   13   16th Division (G).
        "   14   16th Division (Q).
        "   15   Bde. Transport Officer.
        "   16-17   War Diary.
        "   18   File.

S E C R E T.   Copy No 4

49th Inf. Bde. Order No. 189.

Ref. Map Sheets 57.C)   4th December 1917.
     and 62.J)1/40,000

1.   The 49th Inf. Bde. Group will march tomorrow, 5th
     December 1917, to TINCOURT AREA according to attached table.

2.(a) Regulation halts - i.e. from every 50 minutes to the
      clock hour - will be observed.

  (b) Distances as follows will be kept :-

      200 yards between units.
  (c) First line transport will march with units.
3.   Billeting Parties (as laid down in Bde. Order No. 188)
      will report to Staff Captain at Town Major's Office, TINCOURT
      at 11 a.m.
      Maps as above must be taken.

4.   Dinners will be cooked enroute and served out on arrival
      in camp.

5.   Supply Wagons will march with 144th Coy, A.S.C.

6.   Motor lorries for blankets have been asked for. Guides
      from units will report at Brigade H.Q. at 7 a.m. tomorrow to
      conduct same to units' camps. When filled these lorries should
      go to TINCOURT and report to Staff Captain at Town Major's
      Office.

7.   Camps must be left scrupulously clean, but no rear
      parties will be left for handing over.

8.   Brigade H.Q. will close at BARASTRE at 8.45 a.m.
      Reports to head of column while on march.
      Brigade H.Q. will open in TINCOURT area on arrival.
9.   The 155th Field Coy, R.E. will join rear of column
      as it passes through ROCQUIGNY about 10.33 a.m. and will
      continue on the march under orders of G.O.C. 49th Inf. Bde.
      A billeting party of 8 N.C.O's on cycles will report to Staff
      Captain as detailed in para 3.

10. ACKNOWLEDGE.

                                            Captain,
                                A/Brigade Major, 49th Infantry Brigade.

Issued through signals at 10.30 p.m.

Copy No. 1 to G. O. C.   14 to Bde. Sig. Officer.
  "   2   Staff Captain.   15   Bde. Int. Officer.
  "   3   2nd R.Irish Regt.   16   16th Div. (G).
  "   4   7th(S.I.H)R.I.Regt.   17   16th Div. (Q).
  "   5   7/8th R. Innis.Fus.   18   17th Inf. Bde.
  "   6   7/8th R.Irish Fus.   19   18th Inf. Bde.
  "   7   49th M.G.Company.   20   A.D.M.S. 16th Div.
  "   8   49th T.M.Battery.   21   16th Div. Train.
  "   9   155th Field Coy,R.E.   22-23 War Diary.
  "   10   157th Field Coy,R.E.   24   File.
  "   11   144th Coy, A.S.C.
  "   12   115th Field Amb.
  "   13   Bde. Transport Off.

LARGE TABLE TO ACCOMPANY BRIGADE ORDER NO. 1

UNIT.	STARTING POINT.	TIME.	ROUTE.	REMARKS.
186. H.Q.		9 a.m.	O.21.b.3.1. — C.27.a.7.7. — BROQUIGNY — BRESSIL-EN-ARROUAISE — U.6.c.1.6. — U.11.b.5.2 — IMAMCOURT — LOISALLIE — TIFFLEUX-LA-FORET — J.4.c.5.5. — J.16.a.5.2.	Ball-ting Guides will meet Units en Route.
7/R.Irish Regt.		9.5 a.m.		
2/R.Irish Regt.		9.15 a.m.		
7/8 R.Irish Fus.		9.25 a.m.		
7/8 R.Innis.Fus.		9.35 a.m.		
157 Fd.Coy. R.E.		9.45 a.m.		
49th T.M.Coy.		9.50 a.m.		
49th Tr.M.B.		10.5 a.m.		
113 Fd.Amb.		10.10 a.m.		
144 Coy. A.S.C.		10.15 a.m.		

Starting Point: Q.15.d.5.5.

SECRET.   Copy No. 4

49th Inf. Bde. Order No. 190.

5th December 1917.

Ref. Map Sheet 62.C Scale 1/40,000.

1. (a) The 16th Division (less Artillery) is to relieve 55th Division (less Artillery) in the line from P.2.a.0.0 to the MALASSISE ROAD inclusive. Relief to be complete by 10 a.m. December 7th, when command of the front will pass to G.O.C. 16th Division with Headquarters at VILLERS FAUCON.

   (b) The 49th Inf. Bde. will move tomorrow, 6.12.17, as detailed in Table attached, to STE. EMELIE and front line area.

2. Distances as follows to be observed:-

   200 yards between Companies and similar units.
   200 yards between units transport.

3. One blanket will be carried on the man. Instructions re second blanket will be issued later.

4. Billeting parties will report to Staff Captain at the present Brigade H.Q. in STE.EMELIE at 9 a.m.

5. Supply Wagons filled will report to units at 9.30 a.m. and will march with each units' transport to destination where rations will be immediately offloaded and wagons sent back to 144th Coy, A.S.C.

6. R.E. and Medical Reliefs will be carried out under arrangements to be made by C.R.E. and A.D.M.S. respectively.

7. All working parties, guards, anti-aircraft defences, maps, defence schemes, ammunition including S.O.S. Signals and reserve rations will be taken over. A list of all ammunition, showing locations of dumps, will be sent at once to Staff Captain, Brigade Headquarters.

8. Brigade H.Q. close at TINCOURT at 10.30 a.m. and reopen on arrival at STE. EMELIE.

9. ACKNOWLEDGE (stating time of receipt).

                                                     Captain,
                           A/Brigade Major, 49th Infantry Brigade.

Issued through Signals at 11 a.m.

Copy No. 1 to G.O.C.   14 to C.R.E.
"   2   Staff Captain.   15   A.D.M.S.
"   3   2nd R.Irish Regt.   16   112th Field Ambulance.
"   4   7th (S.I.H) R.I.Regt. 17   155th Field Coy,R.E.
"   5   7/8th R. Innis Fus.   18   55th Division.
"   6   7/8th R.Irish Fus.   19   47th Inf. Bde.
"   7   49th M.G.Company.   20   48th Inf. Bde.
"   8   49th T.M.Battery.   21   164th Inf. Bde.
"   9   157th Field Coy,R.E.   22   Bde. Transport Officer.
"   10   144th Coy,A.S.C.   23   Bde. Signal Officer.
"   11   113th Field Amb.   24   Bde. Int. Officer.
"   12   16th Div. (G)   25+26 War Diary.
"   13   16th Div. (Q)   27   File.

TABLE TO ACCOMPANY 49th Inf. Bde. Order No. 100.

Unit.	Starting Point.	Time.	Route.	Remarks.
Brigade H.Q. (less T'port) 9th M.G. Company. (less T'port) 2nd R.Irish Regt. (less T'port)	J.18.d.8.3. do. do.	10.30 a.m. 10.35 a.m. 10.40 a.m.	By lorries via ROISEL - STE.EMELIE to E.33.c.5.0. where units will debus on north side of road facing lorries.	Units to be detailed before marching off from unit grounds into lorry loads of 25 each.
7/8th R.Irish Fus. (less T'port) 7th (S.I.H.)A.I.Rgt. (less T'port) 49th T.M.Battery.	J.18.d.8.3. do. do.	11.15 a.m. 11.25 a.m. 11.35 a.m.	By march route via BARQUAIX - ROISEL - K.16.b.3.3 - VILLERS-FAUCON to E.33.d.9.4. here billeting guides will meet units.	
49th M.G.Coy. T'port 2nd R.Irish Regt. T'port. Brigade H.Q. T'port. 7/8th R.Irish Fus. T'port. 7th (S.I.H.)A.I.Rgt. T'port. 7/8th R.Innis.Fus. T'port.	J.18.d.8.3. do. do. do. do. do.	11.40 a.m. 11.50 a.m. 12.10 p.m. 12.15 p.m. 12.25 p.m. 12.35 p.m.	Via BARQUAIX - ROISEL - K.16.b.3.3 to VILLERS FAUCON.	Under command of Bde. Transport Officer.
7/8th R.Innis.Fus. (less T'port)	J.18.d.8.3.	2.40 p.m.	By lorries via ROISEL - STE.EMELIE to E.33.c.5.0. where unit will debus on North side of road facing lorries	Units to be detailed before marching off from unit ground to lorry loads of 25 each.

SECRET.   Copy No. 3

49th Inf. Bde. Order No. 192.

7th December 1917.

Ref. Maps Sheets 57.c.S.E.
                62.c.N.E.
     1/20,000.

1. The 7th (S.I.H) R.Irish Regt. will relieve the 1st R. Dublin Fus. in the Left Subsection of the SECTOR held by the 48th Inf. Bde. tonight (7th/8th Decr. 1917). Arrangements will be made between C.O's concerned.

2. The head of the 7th (S.I.H) R.I.Regt. is to be at the road junction F.10.c.35.60 (Sheet 62.c.N.E) by 8 p.m. where guides from 1st R. Dublin Fus will meet them.

3. All trench stores, periscopes, gum boots, ammunition and grenades will be carefully taken over and list of same will be forwarded to Brigade H.Q. by 6 p.m. 8th December 1917.

4. Completion of relief to be reported to 48th and 49th Inf. Bde. H.Q. by the code word "POINTER".

5. On completion of relief the command of the portion held by the 7th (S.I.H) R.I.Regt. will pass to G.O.C. 49th Inf. Bde.

6. ACKNOWLEDGE.

                                                          Captain,

A/Brigade Major, 49th Infantry Brigade.

Issued through Signals   p.m.

        Copy No. 1 to G. O. C.
            "   2   48th Inf. Bde.
            "   3   7th (S.I.H) R.I.Regt.
            "   4   File.

SECRET.   Copy No. 4

49th INF. BDE. ORDER NO. 197.

11th Decr. 1917.

Ref. Maps Sheets 57.c.S.E.
                62.c.N.E.
     1/20,000.

1. The 47th Inf. Bde. (less M.G.Company) is relieving the 48th Inf. Bde. (less M.G.Company) in the Right Section of the Divisional Front from F.24.a.0.0 to F.11.a.8.6 on the night 11th/12th December 1917.

2. The following reliefs will be carried out on the night of the 12th/13th December 1917:-

   (a) 7/8th R. Innis Fus. will relieve 2nd R. Irish Regt. in the Front line from F.11.a.8.6 to F.4.d.8.9, and the 7th (S.I.H) R. Irish Regt. from F.4.d.8.9 to the MALASSISE FARM - CATELET COPSE ROAD (inclusive).

   (b) The 2nd R. Irish Regt. will relieve the two Companies of 7/8th R. Irish Fus. - MALASSISE FARM and ground to the S.E. The one Company of the 6th Leicester Regt. in support from F.8.a.6.7 to F.1.b.8.0 will also be relieved by two platoons of the 2nd R. Irish Regt.

   (c) The 7/8th R. Irish Fus. will relieve the 9th Leicester Regt. now situated in the Right Subsection of the 110th Inf. Bde. Front from the MALASSISE FARM - CATELET COPSE ROAD (exclusive) to a line through X.28.b.0.8 - X.27. central - X.27.c.0.6 - X.26.d.0.0 - F.2.a.0.5 (this line being the Northern Boundary of the 16th Div. with the 21st Division). Battalion H.Q. at F.1.b.75.80.

3. Arrangements for relief to be made between C.O's concerned.

4. After relief, the 49th Inf. Bde. will be disposed as follows :-

   Brigade Headquarters at STE. EMILIE.

   7/8th R. Innis Fus. Front line from F.11.a.8.6 to MALASSISE FARM - CATELET COPSE ROAD (inclusive).

   7/8th R. Irish Fus. Front line from MALASSISE FARM - CATELET COPSE ROAD (exclusive) to the Northern Boundary of Div. Front (see para. 2 (c)).

   2nd R. Irish Regt. In support along EPEHY - LEMPIRE RIDGE, with two Companies in the area SANDBAG ALLEY, ZEBRA and YAK POSTS, ELFER COPSE and MAY COPSE, and two Companies in the area OLD COPSE, MALASSISE FARM and ground to N.W.

   7th (S.I.H) R.I.Regt. in Brigade Reserve at STE. EMILIE.

   49th M.G.Company. In line.
   49th T.M.Battery. In line.

5. (a) All trench stores, periscopes (if any), gum boots, ammunition, etc, to be carefully handed and taken over; A return of same to reach this office by 6 p.m. 14th instant.

   (b) All work in hand and proposed will be carefully handed over in writing.

6. On completion of their relief the 7th (S.I.H) R.I.Regt. will move to billets in STE. EMILIE.

7. Completion of relief will be wired to Brigade H.Q. by code words as follows :-

   Relief 2 (a). By both units concerned - "PRESUME".

   " 2 (b). By 2nd R. Irish Regt. - "ASSUME".

   " 2 (c). By 7/8th R. Irish Fus. - "CONSUME".

8. 7th (S.I.H) R.I.Regt. will report their arrival in STE. EMILIE by code word "PICCADILLY".

9. On completion of relief 2(c) the command of that portion of the front will pass from G.O.C. 110th Inf. Bde. to G.O.C. 49th Inf. Bde.

10. ACKNOWLEDGE.

Bowen.

Captain,
A/Brigade Major, 49th Infantry Brigade.

Issued through Signals.

Copy No. 1 to G. O. C.
.. 2   Staff Captain.
.. 3   2nd R. Irish Regt.
.. 4   7th (S.I.H) R.Irish Regt.
.. 5   7/8th R. Innis Fus.
.. 6   7/8th R. Irish Fus.
.. 7   49th M.G.Company.
.. 8   49th T.M.Battery.
.. 9   Bde. Transport Officer.
.. 10   Bde. Int. Officer.
.. 11   Bde. Sig. Officer.
.. 12   157th Field Coy, R.E.
.. 13   144th Coy, A.S.C.
.. 14   113th Field Ambulance.
.. 15   16th Division (G).
.. 16   16th Division (Q).
.. 17   16th Div. Artillery.
.. 18   D.M.G.O.
.. 19   C.R.E.
.. 20   A.D.M.S.
.. 21   21st Division.
.. 22   110th Inf. Bde.
.. 23   47th Inf. Bde.
.. 24   48th Inf. Bde.
.. 25   Left Group R.F.A.
.. 26-27 War Diary.
.. 28   File.

SECRET.   Copy No ....

49th INF. BDE. ORDER No. 199.

16th December 1917.

Ref. Maps 57.c.S.E.
        62.c.N.E.
   1/20,000.

1. (a) 48th Inf. Bde. (less M.G.Company) will relieve 49th Inf. Bde. (less M.G.Company) in the Left Section of Div. Front from F.11.a.8.6 to X.26.d.50.45 on the night 17th/18th December.

    (b) In accordance with above, reliefs, as per table below, will take place, unit commanders concerned being responsible for arranging guides and other details of reliefs.

RELIEF TABLE.

Unit.	Relieved by	Location.
7/8th R.Innis Fus.	2nd R. Dublin Fus.	Right Subsection from F.11.a.8.6 to MALASSISE Fm. Rd. (inclusive).
7/8th R. Irish Fus.	1st R. Dublin Fus.	Left Subsection from MALASSISE Fm. Rd (exclusive) to X.26.d.50.45.
2nd R.Irish Regt.	10th R.Dub. Fus.	In support in MALASSISE FM Area., and in ZEBRA & YAK POSTS.
7th (S.I.H)R.I.Rgt.	8/9th R.Dub.Fus.	In Bde. Reserve in STE. EMILIE.
49th T.M.Battery.	48th T.M.Battery.	

2. All (a) Trench Stores, (b) Ammunition, (c) Written Defence Schemes, (d) Written schemes of work in progress and proposed, and all other documents connected with the line will be carefully handed over to relieving units, and receipts taken for same.

    Copies of (c) and (d) to reach Bde. H.Q. by noon 17th, and of (a) and (b) (with receipts) by 6 p.m. 18th.

3. (a) Completion of relief will be wired by code as under to Brigade Headquarters in the form of a message in reply to one numbered "B.M.C. 535".

2nd R. Irish Regt.	"NIL RETURN".
7th (S.I.H)R.I.Regt.	"NONE TO RECOMMEND".
7/8th R. Innis Fus.	"VACANCIES ALLOTTED".
7/8th R.Irish Fus.	"1483 Sgt G. BAKER".
49th T.M.Battery.	"2466 Cpl T. WILSON".

    (b) Brigade H.Q. REPORT CENTRE will close at STE. EMILIE on completion of relief and will reopen at same hour at HAMEL (J.18.d.8.1).

4. On relief the 49th Inf. Bde. will move back into DIV. RESERVE in HAMEL-TINCOURT Area, according to attached Move Table.

5. ACKNOWLEDGE.

                                                    Captain,

Brigade Major, 49th Infantry Brigade.

Issued through Signals.

Copy No. 1 to G. O. C.
" 2   Staff Captain.
" 3   Asst. Staff Captain.
" 4   Bde. Int. Officer.
" 5   Bde. Signal Officer.
" 6   Bde. Transport Officer.
" 7   2nd R. Irish Regt.
" 8   7th (S.I.H) R.I. Regt.
" 9   7/8th R. Innis Fus.
" 10   7/8th R. Irish Fus.
" 11   49th M.G. Company.
" 12   49th T.M. Battery.
" 13   157th Field Coy, R.E.
" 14   144th Coy, A.S.C.
" 15   113th Field Ambulance.
" 16   16th Div. (G).
" 17   16th Div. (Q).
" 18   16th Div. Artillery.
" 19   D.M.G.O.
" 20   C.R.E.
" 21   A.D.M.S.
" 22   47th Inf. Bde.
" 23   48th Inf. Bde.
" 24   21st Division.
" 25   110th Inf. Bde.
" 26   Left Group R.F.A.
" 27-28 War Diary.
" 29   File.

MOVE TABLE TO ACCOMPANY 49TH INF. BDE. ORDER No. 199.

UNIT.	From.	To.	Remarks.
Brigade Headquarters	STE. EMILIE.	HAMEL J.18.d.8.1.	By march.
7th (S.I.H) R.Irish Regt.	STE. EMILIE.	BUIRE.	By march. Dinners to be cooked enroute and had on arrival at destination. 200 yards distance between Companies and between rear Coy. and Transport.
2nd R. Irish Regt.	Support.	TINCOURT.	By train. Instructions re entraining and detraining points, times, etc. issued later by Staff Captain.
7/8th R. Innis Fus.	Right Subsection.	do.	do.
7/8th R. Irish Fus.	Left Subsection.	do.	do.
49th T.M.Battery.	Line.	do.	do.

SECRET. Copy No 26

49th INF. BDE. ORDER NO. 200.

20th December 1917.

1. The 49th Inf. Bde. will relieve the 47th Inf. Bde. in the Right Section on the 23rd December in accordance with attached table.
   All details will be arranged between Officers Commanding units concerned.

2. The following will be carefully taken over by relieving units:-
   (a) Trench Stores.
   (b) Ammunition and Grenades.
   (c) Written Defence Schemes.
   (d) Written schemes of work in progress & proposed.
   (e) All maps and other documents connected with the line.

   Copies of (a) and (b) will be forwarded to Brigade H.Q. by 6 p.m. 24th December.

3. Advance parties, to include snipers, observers and Nos. 1 of Lewis Gun Teams will take over during daylight and will proceed by march routs.

4. A map showing dispositions of battalions will be forwarded to Brigade Headquarters by 6 p.m. 24th December.

5. 49th Inf. Bde. H.Q. will close at HAMEL and reopen at STE. EMILIE on completion of relief.

6. Completion of reliefs will be reported by wire by the code word "SALVAGE".

7. ACKNOWLEDGE.

I. L. MacDonald. Captain,

Brigade Major, 49th Infantry Brigade.

Issued through Signals.

Copy No.	Unit			
1	to G.O.C.	15	to	16th Division (G).
2	Staff Captain.	16		16th Division (Q).
3	Bde. Int. Officer.	17		16th Div. Artillery.
4	Bde. Sig. Officer.	18		D.M.G.O.
5	Bde. T'port Officer.	19		C. R. E.
6	2nd R. Irish Regt.	20		A.D.M.S.
7	7th (SIH) R.Irish Regt.	21		47th Inf. Bde.
8	7/8th R. Innis Fus.	22		48th Inf. Bde.
9	7/8th R. Irish Fus.	23		24th Division.
10	49th M.G. Company.	24		Left Bde. 24th Div.
11	49th T.M. Battery.	25		Right Group R.F.A.
12	157th Field Coy, R.E.	26-27		War Diary.
13	144th Coy, A.S.C.	28		File.
14	113th Field Amb.			

RELIEF TABLE TO ACCOMPANY 49TH INF. BDE. ORDER NO. 220.

Relieving Unit.	Unit to be relieved.	Location.	Remarks.
2nd R. Irish Regt.	6th R. Irish Regt.	Right Subsection.	Relieving unit not to be East of LESIRE before 5.30 p.m. to proceed by train leaving TINCOURT siding at 5 p.m. (M.17.c).
7th (SIR) R. Irish Regt.	6th Connaught Rangers.	Left Subsection.	By march route. Relieving unit not to be East of LESIRE before 5 p.m.
7/8th R. Innis Fus.	1st R. Munster Fus.	Support. LEMPIRE.	By train leaving TINCOURT siding at 4.30 p.m. Relieving unit not to enter LEMPIRE before 6 p.m. One Company to proceed by train leaving 3 p.m.
7/8th R. Irish Fus.	7th Leinster Regt.	Reserve. STE. EMILIE.	By march route. Relief to be complete by 1 p.m.
6th T.M.Battery.	47th T.M.Battery.	Right Section.	By march route under arrangements to be made by O.C. 48th T.M. Battery.
49th Inf. Bde.H.Q.	48th Inf. Bde. H.Q.	STE. EMILIE.	Move to be arranged by Staff Captain.

NOTE.- All movement East of STE. EMILIE will be by platoons at 5 minutes interval.
Units will report at the train 15 minutes before time of starting.

SECRET.   Copy No :.16.

49th INF. BDE. ORDER No: 201.

27th December 1915.

1. The 7/8th R. Innis Fus. will relieve the 2nd R. Irish Regt. and the 7/8th R. Irish Fus. will relieve the 7th (SIH) R. Irish Regt. in the Right and Left Subsections of the Right Section respectively on the night December 29th/30th.

2. On completion of relief the 2nd R. Irish Regt. will proceed to Brigade Reserve in STE. EMILIE and the 7th (SIH) R. Irish Regt. to Brigade Support in LEMPIRE and RONSSOY.

3. Advance parties, to include snipers, observers and Nos. 1 of Lewis Gun Teams will proceed by daylight to take over. Taking over parties from units being relieved will report at Support and Reserve Battalion H.Q. by 8 p.m. 29th instant.

4. Order of relief will be as follows :-

7/8th R. Irish Fus. will not be East of LEMPIRE before 4.30 p.m. Their leading two Companies will relieve the two back Companies of the 7th (SIH) R. Irish Regt, who will at once relieve two Companies of the 7/8th R. Innis Fus. in the LEMPIRE DEFENCES. As soon as latter relief is complete, the 7/8th R. Innis Fus. will commence to relieve the 2nd R. Irish Regt. Officers Commanding Battalions will maintain touch with their Companies during the relief. All movement will be by platoons at 500 yards interval.

5. All other details will be arranged between Commanding Officers concerned.

6. The following will be carefully handed and taken over:-

    (a) Trench Stores.
    (b) Defence arrangements.
    (c) Work in progress and proposed.
    (d) Working Parties.

R.S.M.
12-noon
Copies of (a) and (c) to reach Brigade H.Q. by 4 p.m. 30th instant.

7. Completion of relief in front line will be notified to Brigade H.Q. by code word "MARGARINE".
7th (SIH) R. Irish Regt. and 2nd R. Irish Regt. will notify Brigade H.Q. when they arrive in Support and Reserve respectively by code word "BUTTER".

8. The 18th Inf. Bde. is being relieved by 17th Inf. Bde. on the night December 29th/30th.

9. ACKNOWLEDGE.

                        A.G. MacDonald, Captain.
                        Brigade Major, 49th Infantry Brigade.

Issued through Signals.

Copy No. 1 to G.O.C.   12 to 14th Coy, A.S.C.
"   2   Staff Captain.   13   113th Field Amb.
"   3   Bde. Sig. Officer.   14   16th Division (G).
"   4   Bde. Int. Officer.   15   16th Division (Q).
"   5   2nd R.Irish Rgt.   16   16th Div. Artillery.
"   6   7th (SIH) R.Irish Rgt. 17   D.A.G.O.
"   7   7/8th R. Innis Fus.   18 LEFT Right Bde. 24th Div.
"   8   7/8th R. Irish Fus.   19   47th Inf. Bde.
"   9   49th M.G. Company.   20   48th Inf. Bde.
"   10   49th T.M.Battery.   21   Right Group.
"   11   155th Field Coy, R.E. 22-23 War Diary.
                                  24   File.

WAR DIARY,

FOR MONTH OF JANUARY, 1918.

VOLUME :- H.

UNIT :- 7th (S.I.H.) R. Irish Regiment.

WAR DIARY
or
INTELLIGENCE SUMMARY
(Erase heading not required.)

Army Form C. 2118.

JANUARY 1918

Instructions regarding War Diaries and Intelligence Summaries are contained in F. S. Regs., Part II. and the Staff Manual respectively. Title pages will be prepared in manuscript.

Place	Date JAN.	Hour	Summary of Events and Information	Remarks and references to Appendices
RONSSOY	1		Visibility very good - numerous German aeroplanes came over. Working parties of 1 offr and 45 men per Coy were supplied to R.E. They were seen whenever shelled. The village was vigorously shelled all day	A/1/42
	2		A quiet day until this evening when LEMPIRE RD and RONSSOY village were heavily shelled from 6 to 8 pm again between 9 and 10 pm. Retaliation asked for & given at 10.15 pm.	A/1/42
	3		Apart from air activity - a very quiet day	A/1/42
	4		Slightly foggy which interfered with air activity. - Battn was relieved by 8/9 R Scots Fusiliers. Battn withdrew to ST EMILIE and proceeded to "billets" at TINCOURT. (Copy of Operation order att'd)	A/1/42
	5		2nd whole of the Battn had Baths at MARQUAIX	A/1/42
	6		Working party of 6 offr and 200 OR supplied for wiring under R.E. Lieut. BRENNAN RONSSOY. Sig Sergt Bolton presented with Military Medal by Gen Jeudwine	A/1/42
	7		All Coys respirators inspected. Dinner dance for the men in Divisional TINCOURT.	A/1/42
	8		Training of Lewis Gunners continued. P.T & Swedish games - Bayonet fighting	A/1/42
	9		Training as in previous day. All Box respirators inspected by Brit Gas P.L.O.	A/1/42
	10		Proceeded by train to ST EMILIE and marched to relieve the 6th Loam. Rangers in the Right Sub-section of the Left Section. The relief was carried out without incident (4th S. Br.)	A/1/42
	11		Quiet day — Small activity. A patrol of 1 off'r & 35 O.R. was sent out & patrolled the district round LITTLE PRIEL FARM & the valley to the S.East but the enemy were not seen	A/1/42
	12		Quiet day. 2 Patrols of 1 offr & 10 OR each sent out at night for 3 hrs. Enemy not encountered.	A/1/42
	13		Great aerial activity - hostile shelling of HEYTHROP POST and THE NEST. 3 Patrols sent out at night, consists of 1 offr & 20 men, 1 offr & 10 men, & 1 offr & 10 men. The enemy were not encountered.	A/1/42
	14		Quiet day. Front line trenches intermittently shelled and retaliation obtained. Three patrols (1 offr & 20, 1 offr & 5, 1 offr & 12) sent out at night. No enemy encountered	A/1/42
	15		Front line trenches shelled during morning and retaliation obtained. Three patrols were sent to the field wire in particular those in HEYTHROP LANE. A patrol of 1 offr & 20 men went out at night, but no enemy was encountered	A/1/42

AMK Carpenter
Capt & Adjt

WAR DIARY
or
INTELLIGENCE SUMMARY.

(Erase heading not required.)

Army Form C. 2118.

Place	Date JAN	Hour	Summary of Events and Information	Remarks and references to Appendices
In the field	16		Quiet day. Front line Coys in dugouts on slopes in front being at night. 7/8 Royal Innis. Relieved Batt. and marched to Peronne. Board fires at STE EMILIE (copy of operation order attached)	appx 1
	17		Heavy rain fell. Cleaning and checking of arms and equipment. Working parties supplied. Strength + 20 men to Brigade + 1 R.E. + 2/Lt. O.R. + 180 innuiling Coys. Working in shifts of 4 hours.	appx 2
	18		Batt. had baths at VILLERS FAUCON. Working parties supplied – 1 Sgt + 10 O.R. to Brigade H.Q + Work parties to 150 innuiling Coy. Town mayor.	appx 2
	19		Quiet day. Usual working parties supplied. Practical inspection carried out.	appx 2
	20		Church services at VILLERS FAUCON	appx 2
	21		Usual working parties. Raid practised.	appx 2
	22		Relieved 7/8 Royal Innis. Fus. in the Right Subsection of the Left Section Relief in Reserve line started over to 7/8 R. Innis Fus. (copy of operation order attached)	appx 2
	23		Intermittent shelling of all parts of the Batt. area. Patrols of 1 Officer + 9 O.R. was sent out and obtained much valuable information.	appx 2
	24		Quiet day. Visibility poor. Small patrols out in early morning. Working parties supplied + R.E	appx 2
	25		Enemy barrage were put down on HEYTHROP POST at 4:30am. S.O.S signal were given and our barrage opened at 4:40 am. No infantry attack followed. A listening patrol of 1 N.C.O + 6 O.R in LITTLE PRIEL FARM saw an enemy patrol and fired on them. Our patrol returned, but one man (the N.C.O) is missing. Our Artillery shelled the vicinity of LARK POST AND EAGLE QUARRY and damaged the wire.	appx 2
	26		Visibility bad owing to heavy mist. Much wiring carried on on the whole front. Contemplated raid postponed.	appx 2

A.M.R. Lawson
Capt + Adjt

Army Form C. 2118.

WAR DIARY
or
INTELLIGENCE SUMMARY.
(Erase heading not required.)

Instructions regarding War Diaries and Intelligence Summaries are contained in F. S. Regs., Part II. and the Staff Manual respectively. Title pages will be prepared in manuscript.

Place	Date JAN	Hour	Summary of Events and Information	Remarks and references to Appendices
In the field	27.		Heavy mist until the afternoon when it began to lift. Much work done on improving the posts. Quiet day.	AWS
	28.		Visibility good, much aerial activity. Battalion relieved by 7/8th R. Innis. Fusiliers and moved into Brigade Support (Coy in Vaulx trench) (Coy in Sugar trench).	AWS
	29.		Working parties supplied to R.E. at night. Quiet day.	AWS
	30.		Working parties supplied. Much aerial activity. Both Commenced.	AWS
	31.		Visibility low owing to fog. Some intermittent shelling of area. Continues.	AWS

AWK Lawson
Capt & Adjt

for Lt. Col. Comdg. Y.K. (S.W.) R.I. Regt.

SECRET.   Copy No. 12
              Operation Order No. 52 by Lt. Col. H.E. Norton
              Comdg. SOUTH IRISH HORSE, (7th R.I. Rgt.)
                          9th January 1918.

1.   The 49th Infantry Brigade will relieve the 47th Inf. Bde in the LEFT SECTION of the Divnl. Front on the night of the 10/11th January.

2.   The Battalion will relieve the 6th Connaught Rangers in the RIGHT SUBSECTION. Companies will relieve in the following order :-

      "A" Coy S.I.H. will relieve "C" Coy 6th Conn. Rangers.
      "B" "   "   "   "   "B" "   "   "   "
      "S" "   "   "   "   "D" "   "   "   "
      "C" "   "   "   "   "A" "   "   "   "
      Hd. Qrs. "   "   "   Hd. Qrs. "   "   "

3.   Advance party consisting of Capt. Wardell, 1 Offr. & 1 N.C.O. per Coy. Regimental Gas N.C.O., Signal Sergt., Nos. 1 of Lewis Gun teams, Cook Sergt. Acting R.S.M., Cpl. Rodman and 4 scouts will parade outside Orderly Room at 9.30am and proceed to take over in daylight. Guides will be met at Battalion H.Q. at 12 Noon.

4.   Coys. will entrain as follows from TINCOURT :-

           "S" Coy. at 3.pm.
           "A" "B" & "C" Coys at 4.pm.

      No Coy. will be E. of EPEHY-LEMPIRE RD. before 5.30pm.
      Coys will report at entraining siding 15 minutes before time of starting.
      The STE EMILIE-RONSSOY RD. East of road junction at F.19.b.60.90 WILL NOT BE USED.
      All movement E. of STE EMILIE will be by platoons at five minutes interval.
      Lewis Guns and 24 drums per gun will be taken with Coys. and not sent up by Transport.
      Each man will carry one blanket.

5.   The route from STE EMILIE will be via EMILIE-RONSSOY RD. as far as F.19.b.59 where they will proceed by the track through F.14.
      Guides for main bodies will be met for "A" "B" & "C" Coys. at Battalion H.Q. F.10.c.24 and for "S" Coy at F.11.a.93.

6.   Defence schemes and all documents connected with the line with the exception of aeroplane photographs - all work in progress and proposed (in writing) - Trench Stores, Ammunition and Grenades will be carefully taken over. Copies of Trench Store receipts will be handed in to Battn. H.Q. by 12.Noon on 11th inst.

7.   Completion of relief will be notified to Battn. H.Q. by the words "Double Rum Issue"

8.   TRANSPORT - Officers spare kits - all blankets over and above 1 per man, tightly rolled in bundles of 10 and all other material for Transport Lines will be dumped outside Battn. H.Q. by 10. am.
      Baggage wagons will be available for this transport. R.S.M. will detail a guard from the Band to remain until the dump is removed by the quartermaster.
      The Transport Offr. will detail the following transport to report at 1.pm :- Per Coy. 1 limber at Coy. H.Q. - Per H.Q. 1 limber, Maltese Cart and Mess Cart, at Battn. H.Q.

9.   ACKNOWLEDGE.

                                              (sd) A.H.D. Lawson
                                                   Capt. & Adjt.
Copies to.
1-4 - O.C. Coys.   8 - M.O.
5 - 6th Conn. Rgrs.   9 - Tport Off.
6 - 49th Inf. Bde.   10 - R.S.M.
7 - Sig. Offr.   11 - War Diary.
                        12 - File.

SECRET   Operation Order No. 53 by Lt.Col. H.E. Norton   Copy No. 13
           Comdg. SOUTH IRISH HORSE (7th R.I.Rgt.)
                         15th Jan. 1918.

1. The Battn. will be relieved on the night of the 16th Jan. 1918 by the 7/8 R. Inniskilling Fus. and on relief will march by platoons at 5 minutes interval to Brigade Reserve line in cutting at STE EMILIE.

2. Companies will be relieved as follows :-
    "A" Coy will be relieved by "D" Coy R. Innis. Fus.
    "B" " "   "   " "C" " "   "   "
    "C" " "   "   " "B" " "   "   "
    "S" " "   "   " "A" " "   "   "
    H.Q. "   "   "   H.Q.
Completion of relief will be notified to Battn. H.Q. by words "No vacancy desired"

3. The following will be carefully handed over and receipts obtained :-
    (a) Trench Stores.
    (b) Defence arrangements and all information about the line, except aeroplane photographs.
    (c) Work in progress and work proposed (in writing)
    (d) Working parties.
    (e) Ammunition and grenades.
Copies of (a) and (e) will be handed in to Orderly Room by 11.0am on the 17th inst.

4. Guides of 1 per Coy will meet advance party R. Innis. Fus. will report at Battn. H.Q. at 12.0noon on the 16th inst.
    Guides for main body R. Innis. Fus. will be provided as under :-
    1 guide per platoon from "A" "B" & "C" Coys will report at Battn. H.Q. at 5.0pm.
    1 guide per platoon from "S" Coy will be at F.11.a.93 at 5.0pm.

5. The route to STE EMILIE will be by the track through F.14.

6. Major Furlong and the four C.Q.M. Sergts. will report to Battn. H.Q. R. Innis. Fus at 2.0pm to take over billets.

7. Transport Officer will detail the following transport :-
    For "S" Coy 1 limber at junction of TOMBOIS & LONDON RD. (F.11.a.93)
    For "A" Coy. 1 limber at F.4 Central.
    "   "B" " 1   "   "   "
    "   "C" " 1   "   " Battn. H.Q.
    "   H.Q. 1 limber, Mess Cart, Maltese Cart, & Battn. H.Q.

8. Acknowledge.

                                    (sd) A.H.D. Lawson,
                                        Capt & Adjt.

Copies to :-
    1   49th Inf. Bde.
    2 - 5 Coy. Commdrs.
    6   7/8 R. Innis. Fus.
    7   Major Furlong.
    8   M.O.
    9   Tpst. Offr.
    10   QrMaster.
    11   Sig. Offr.
    12   R.S.M.
    13   War Diary.
    14   File.

SECRET.   Copy No. 11
                    Operation Order No. 54 by Lt.Col.H.E.Norton,
                       Comdg. SOUTH IRISH HORSE (7th R.I.Rgt.)
                                    21st Jan. 1918.

1.   The Battn. will relieve the 7/8 R.Innis.Fus on the night of
     the 22nd inst. Coys. will relieve in the following order :-
          "A" Coy. S.I.H. will relieve "A" Coy. R.Innis.Fus.
          "B" "   "   "   "   "B" "   "   "
          "C" "   "   "   "   "C" "   "   "
          "S" "   "   "   "   "D" "   "   "
          Hd. Qrs. "   "   "   Hd. Qrs. "   "   "

2.   Advance Party consisting of Major Furlong 1 Officer and one
     N.C.O. per Coy. A/R.S.M. Regtl.Gas N.C.O. Signal Sgt. Nos.1 of
     Lewis Gun teams and Cook Sergt. will parade outside Orderly
     Room at 10.0am and proceed to take over in daylight. Guides
     will be met at R.Innis.Fus. Battn.H.Q. at 12.0 noon.

3.   Order of march for main body will be "A" "B" "C" "S" Coys
     and Hd.Qrs. Coys. will march by platoons at 5 minutes
     interval, leading platoon to march off at 4.0pm.
          Guides for "C" Coy and for "S" Coy (as regards YAK and ZEBRA
     posts) will be at Battn.H.Q. F.10.c.24 at 5.30pm and for "B"
     Coy. at F.11.a.71 at 5.30pm.

4.   The following will be carefully taken over :-
          (a) Trench Stores.
          (b) Defence arrangements and all information about the
              line, except aeroplane photographs.
          (c) Work in progress and proposed (in writing)
          (d) Working Parties.
          (e) S.A.A. and Grenades.
     Copies of receipts will be sent to Battn.H.Q. by 8.0am on
     23rd Jan.

5.   Completion of relief will be notified to Battn. H.Q. by the
     words "Hasten Return G"

6.   Blankets will be tightly rolled in bundles of 10 and dumped
     outside Guard Room by 10.0am. Officers' spare kits will be
     dumped at same place by 12.0noon.

7.   Transport Officer will arrange for collection of stores as
     in para. 6.
          Two limbers per Coy. and 1 per H.Qrs. will report at 3.0pm
     in Battn. HxQxxx Mess Cart will report to Battn.Hd.Qrs. and
     Maltese Cart to M.O. at 3.30pm

8.   Quartermaster will arrange for rations to be carried on
     Coy. limbers.
          Ration and water dumps for following nights are as follows:-

          For "A" Coy. at SANDBAG ALLEY.
           " "C" & "S" Coys at F.4.c.80 on LEMPIRE RD.
           " "B" Coy. at junction of LONDON RD. and TOMBOIS RD.
           " Hd. Qrs. at Battn.Hd.Qrs.

9.   Acknowledge.

                                             (sd) A.H.D.Lawson,
                                                  Capt. & Adjt.
Copies to :-
     1-4   O.C.Coys.
       5   7/8th R.Innis.Fus.
       6   49th Inf.Bde.
       7   Sig.Offr.
       8   M.O.
       9   Tspt.Offr.
      10   R.S.M.
      11   War Diary.
      12   File.

Secret. Operation Order No. 55 by Lt. Col. H.S Norton   Copy No. 11
        Comdg. South Irish Horse (7th R.I. Regt)
                        27th Jan. 1918

1. The Battalion will be relieved in the Front Line on the night of 28th Jan. 1918 by the 7/8 Royal Innis. Fus. and will proceed to Brigade Support

2. "A" Coy will be relieved by "D" Coy R. Innis. Fus.
    "B" "   "   "   "   " "B" "   "   "   "
    "C" "   "   "   "   " "C" "   "   "   "
    "S" "   "   "   "   " "A" "   "   "   "

3. Guides will not be required.

4. Advance party consisting of 1 Officer per Coy & 1 N.C.O. per platoon will proceed to take over Support positions at 12 noon. These N.C.Os will meet their respective platoons at new Battln. H.Q. and act as guides.

5. "C" Coy will proceed to RIDGE RESERVE N F2 Central to about F2 a 24 - Coy HQ at F2 C 25 Vacated by "A" Coy R. Innis. Fus.

   "A" Coy will proceed to L'EMPIRE VILLAGE - 1 platoon in ENFER WOOD - 1 platoon in the village about F15 d 13.
   The platoon in the village will man MAY COPSE.
   One platoon less the Officer will be attached to "B" Coy and be accommodated in OLD COPSE.
   Coy HQ will be at F15 b 13. vacated by "B" Coy R. Innis. Fus.

   "B" Coy will proceed to MALASSISE FARM. 2 platoons will be accommodated in OLD COPSE. These will include the platoon attached from "A" Coy.

   "S" Coy will move to Cutting F2 C 25 - Coy. HQ. in Cutting vacated by "D" Coy. R. Innis. Fus.

   Battalion H.Q. and AID POST will be at F15 b 13.

6. One limber per Coy will report to present ration dumps collect stores and carry to new Coy. H.Q. as follows:-
       For "A" Coy 5.30 p.m.
       " "B" "C" and "S" Coys 6.30 p.m.
   One limber, mess cart and maltese cart will report at Battln. HQ. at 6 p.m.

7. All Trench stores will be most carefully handed over and taken over.
   Both taking over lists will be sent to Battln. H.Q. by 11 am on 29th Jan.

8. Relief complete in present positions will be reported to Battln. H.Q. by the words "Your Orders noted"
   On arrival in Support, Coys will wire to new Battln. H.Q. the words "Rum Plentiful"

9. Rations will be delivered tomorrow and following nights:-
       For "A" Coy (less 1 platoon) and HQ at Battln. HQ at 5/30 p.m.
       " "B" " (plus 1 platoon of "A") - at F. 8 a 63
       " "C" and "S" Coys at entrance of Cutting at F2 C 32
   Water Carts will fill tanks at new Battln HQ at 5/30 p.m. and will deliver to HQrs of "B" "C" & "S" Coys at 7/30 pm

10. Acknowledge.

Copies to.
Nos 1 to 4   Coys.
No. 5   Transport Officer
" 6   Medical Officer
" 7   7/8 R. Innis. Fus.
" 8   49th Inf. Bde.
" 9   Signalling Officer
" 10   Lewis Gun Officer
" 11   War Diary
" 12   R.S.M.

                          (Sd) A.H.D. Lawson
                               Capt. & Adjt.

49/76

WAR DIARY.

FOR MONTH OF FEBRUARY, 1918.

VOLUME :- 5

UNIT :- ML (S.I.H.) Btn. R. Irish Regt.

Army Form C. 2118.

7(S1H) Royal Scots Regt.

WAR DIARY
or
INTELLIGENCE SUMMARY
(Erase heading not required.)

Feb 1918

Instructions regarding War Diaries and Intelligence Summaries are contained in F. S. Regs., Part II. and the Staff Manual respectively. Title Pages will be prepared in manuscript.

Place	Date	Hour	Summary of Events and Information	Remarks and references to Appendices
LAMPINE	Feb 1		In support. Slight shelling. Quite day generally.	
	2nd		" enemy occasionally shelled X rds very quiet.	
	3rd		" " quite day. Relieved by the 1st Royal Scots Fus., relief completed by 3 PM. Batt. entrained at ST EMILIE to billets at HAMEL	
HAMEL	4		Day was spent in cleaning up & sheshing equipment	
	5th		The day was spent. Training football match in the afternoon A+B v C+D	
	6th		Training was carried on Coys A & B firing at Musketry each morn fired 5 rds Grouping 5 application & 10 rapid	
	7		General Sir Hubert de la P. Gough K.C.B. K.C.V.O. visited the Bn presented Medal Ribbons to Officers & other ranks. Two Boys were found to the Guard of Honour	
	8th		Day was spent training all Lewis Gunner fired a practice on the 300 range.	
	9th		The Batt relieved the 2nd Royal Scots Regt. at VILLERS FAUCON relief was completed by 1 P.M.	
VILLERS FAUCON	10th		A working party of three officers & 200 O.R. was working behind RONSSOY wiring position was shelled & Pte Daly & Pte Haugh were wounded	

WAR DIARY or INTELLIGENCE SUMMARY

7e (S14) Royal Irish Regt.

Feb 1918

Army Form C. 2118.

Place	Date	Hour	Summary of Events and Information	Remarks and references to Appendices
VILLERS FAUCON	10"		Upon reorganization of Brigades 8 Officers & 317 O.R. joined from the 6th Royal Irish Regt.	A/A
"	11"		Four Officers & 200 O.R. working on new line of trenches remainder of Batt. training. Officer rendering completion in the afternoon Lt. R.J. Shearer wounded	A/A
"	12"		Training & 200 working party	A/A
"	13"		" " " "	A/A
"	14"		Church Parade and inspection. Batt. presented to the line & relieved the 15th Durham Light Infantry in the left sub-sect of the left sector	A/A
EPEHY LEFT SECT	15"		Very quiet, patrols were sent out.	A/A
"	16		Some shelling in the morning, Pte Peel. Pte Hennessy & Pte Fogarty were wounded while on a working party	A/A
"	17"		Enemy aircraft very active, a low flying machine fired on men of the Batt. wounding C.W. Rodencurch, Pte Belyeked was also wounded	A/A

WAR DIARY
or
INTELLIGENCE SUMMARY

Army Form C. 2118.

7th (S.I.H.) ROYAL IRISH REGT

FEB 1918

Place	Date	Hour	Summary of Events and Information	Remarks and references to Appendices
LEFT SECT	18th		An inter coy relief took place to relieving C & S with "A" slight shelling of front line, when transport was returning, enemy's anti-aircraft dropped a bomb & killed Bgl Lynches, & wounded L/C Mackay Pte Mc Garvey Pte Harkin. One horse had to be destroyed.	A/A
"	19th		Quite day. Enemy artillery patrols were sent with the object of obtaining identification but failed.	A/A
"	20th		" " " " "	A/A
"	21st	5 AM	Enemy put down a barrage on our front-line – the S.O.S was fired & replied to, nothing else happened. Lt. N.d Wolff & with 2/Lt Smythe, Pte Fitzgibbon, Pte Byrne & Pte Rawless were wounded. J. Smythe of the day was quite.	A/A
"	22nd		Day quite, Relieved at night. By the 2nd Batt Royal Irish Regt, relief was completed by 8.30 P.M. Batt went into support in EPEHY	A/A
EPEHY	23rd		& took over the EPEHY Defences very quite day	A/A

J. B. Hunt Capt & adjt
for
LT. COL. COMMANDING
7th (S.I.H.) ROYAL IRISH REGT (7th R. I. REGT)

Army Form C. 2118.

7ᵗʰ (S.I.H.) Royal Irish Regt.

WAR DIARY
or
INTELLIGENCE SUMMARY

FEB 1918

(Erase heading not required.)

Place	Date	Hour	Summary of Events and Information	Remarks and references to Appendices
EPEHY	24ᵗʰ		Some light shelling, working parties found for REDLINE	
"	25ᵗʰ		Very quiet	
"	26ᵗʰ		Some shelling on night in the morning the Bat'n relieved the 7/6 Royal Innis Fus in the Right Sub-Section. relief was completed quietly by 8-30 P.M.	
RIGHT SUB SECT	27ᵗʰ		Quite day some shelling to the right & left of Bat'n H.Q. strong fighting patrols sent out	
"	28ᵗʰ		Back area was shelled slightly in the morning & more heavily in the afternoon. suddenly relieved by the 8ᵗʰ/Bat'n Leicester Regt: proceeded by march route to VILLERS FAUCON & occupied ADRIAN CAMP	

LT. COL. COMMANDING
SOUTH IRISH HORSE (7th R. I. REGT.)

Copy No. 11

OPERATION ORDER NO. 62 BY LIEUT-COL. H.E. NORTON, COMMANDING

SOUTH IRISH HORSE, 7th. R. IRISH REGT.   28-2-18

1. The South Irish Horse will be relieved by the 8th. Battn. Leicester Regt. in the Right Sub Section on the night of 28-2/1-3
   The Battalion on relief will proceed to Billets in VILLERS FAUCON.

2. The following will be carefully handed over :-
   (a) Trench Stores
   (b) Maps and all information concerning the Line, including Aeroplane Photographs.
   (c) Work Done and Proposed (In writing)
   (d) Defence Schemes.
   Trench Store Lists, properly signed and counter-signed, will be forwarded to Battalion H.Q. by 9 a.m. 1-3-18.

3. Advance Parties from the 8th Leicesters will be sent to report to the respective Company H.Q. as they arrive.
   On receipt of the Code Message "777", Coys will send to Battn H.Q., one N.C.O. per Platoon. These N.C.Os will act as Coy Advance Parties and meet their respective Platoons at Railway Crossing (E.23.d.6.2) and act as guides to Billets
   Guides for the relieving Unit, 1 per Platoon will be sent to report to Battn H.Q. at 6-15 p.m.
   Coy. Q.M.S. have been instructed to act on behalf of their Coys at VILLERS FAUCON re Billets etc.

4. One Limber per Company will be available at Battn H.Q. at 6-30pm
   One Limber, Mess Cart and Maltese Cart will be at the disposal of Battn H.Q. at the same hour.

5. Companies will move off as relieved, reporting completion of relief to Battn H.Q. by the Code Message "S.D.V."
   Companies will report arrival in billets to Battn H.Q.

6. Acknowledge.

Capt & Adjt.

Copies to
Nos 1 to 4   Coys
No. 5   8th Leicesters
No. 6   49th Inf Bde.
No. 7.   Transport Officer
No. 8   Intelligence Officer
No. 9   Signalling Officer
No. 10   Medical Officer
No. 11   File
No. 12   War Diary
No. 13   R.S.M.

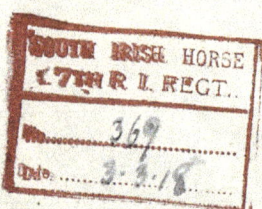

OPERATION ORDERS NO. 61 BY LIEUT-COL. H.E. NORTON, COMMANDING   Copy No. 12

SOUTH IRISH HORSE (7th. R. IRISH REGT.)   25-3-18

---

1. The South Irish Horse will relieve the 7/8th. R. Innis Fus. in the Right Sub Section on the night of 25th/26th, Feby '18 26/27th

   "C" Coy S.I.H. will relieve "D" Coy R. Innis Fus (Left Front)
   "A" "   do   "   "   "B" "   do   (Right Front)
   "B" "   do   "   "   "A" "   do   (Support)
   "S" "   do   "   "   "C" "   do   (Reserve)

   Companies will move off in the following order, starting at 6-30 p.m., with 5 minute interval between Platoons :-
   "C", "A", "B", "S"

2. One Officer per Coy and one N.C.O. per Platoon and No. 1 of Lewis Gun Teams will proceed to the Line at 2 p.m. on 26th., being met by Guides at H.Q. of R. Innis Fus. (F.1.b.7.0)

3. Documents will be taken over as usual.
   Copies of Trench Store List, Work Proposed and in Progress and a List of Maps will be sent to Battn H.Q. by 12 NOON 27th. inst

4. Guides for Companies will be at F.1.c.90.90 at 6-30 p.m.

5. The two Anti-Aircraft Lewis Guns from Brigade Transport Lines will rejoin "C" Coy at 3.0 p.m.

6. Rations will be brought to Battalion H.Q. and dumped there under charge of C.Q.M.S.

7. All Cooking will be done in the Cutting.

8. Water will be carried up in Petrol Tins - 12 per Coy.
   One Water Cart will be left at Battn H.Q. full, and and the Tanks there will be filled.

9. The Intelligence Officer will arrange with "S" Coy for Covering Patrols.

10. Completion of Relief will be notified to Battn H.Q. by the Code Message "WHISKEY RECEIVED"

11. Acknowledge.

(Sd) B.J. Start

Capt & Adjt.

Operation Order No. 60 by Lieut-Col H.E. Norton, Commanding 8th (Irish) Horse 7th R. Irish Regt.
21st Feby 18

1. The South Irish Horse will be relieved by the 2nd Battn. R. Irish Regiment in the Left Sub Section on the night 22nd/23rd Feby 18.
   "A" Coy R. Irish will relieve "S" Coy S.I.H.
   "B"   "   "   "   "A"   "
   "C"   "   "   "   "B"   "
   "D"   "   "   "   "C"   "

2. An Advance Party consisting of 1 Officer and one Gas N.C.O. per Coy and 1 N.C.O. per Platoon will report at Support Battn. H.Q. at 10 a.m. 22nd inst. Battn Gas N.C.O. will accompany this Party and take over Battn H.Q.

3. Guides of 1 per Coy to meet the Advance Party of the 2nd R. Irish will report to Lieut Brewster in Railway Cutting by the R.E.M's Dugout at 12.45 p.m. on 22nd inst.
   Guides of 1 per platoon to meet the main body of the 2nd R. Irish will report to Lieut Brewster at 6.15 p.m. in the same place.

4. O.C. "C" Coy will detail 2 Lewis Guns and Teams to relieve 2 Lewis Gun Teams of the 2nd R. Irish in Brigade Transport Lines by 12 Noon 22nd inst.

5. Companies will take over billets vacated by 2nd R. Irish as follows:
   "S" Coy S.I.H. will take over from "C" Coy R. Irish
   "B" "   "   "   "   "   "D"   "   "
   "A" "   "   "   "   "   "A"   "   "
   "C" "   "   "   "   "   "B"   "   "

6. Rations will be delivered to Cookhouses of Coys etc. in Support Positions at 7 p.m. Coys will each detail one guide to proceed with their Advance Parties and locate Cookhouses in order that they can guide ration limber thereto. These guides will meet Ration limbers at F.H.C. 7.5 at 6.45 p.m. on 22nd inst. O.C. "C" Coy will detail a N.C.O to ensure that guides are at this point at the appointed hour.
   The Transport Officer will detail one limber per Coy for the conveyance of Lewis Guns etc. from present positions to billets in Support. These limbers reporting to Coys at 4.30 p.m. In addition one limber for "A" & "S" Coys and one limber for "B" & "C" Coys will report at Battn H.Q. at 6.15 p.m. where guides will be allotted. These limbers will convey Cooking utensils to Cookhouses in Support.
   One limber, Mess Cart & Maltese Cart will report to Battalion H.Q. at 4.30 p.m.
   Water may only be drawn from Water Point in EPEHY during hours of darkness. Coys will make their own arrangements for running water for cooking purposes, etc.

Sheet 2.

7. The following will be carefully handed over & taken over:-
   (a) Trench Stores
   (b) Information about the line. (Except Aeroplane Photographs)
   (c) Work in progress of repair (in writing).
   (d) Working Parties.

   Ammunition & grenade Returns made up to 12 noon 22nd inst will be rendered to Battn H.Q. by 12 Noon on 22nd inst.

   Trench Store lists properly signed & countersigned & will be forwarded to Battn H.Q. on completion of relief.

8. O.C. 2nd R. Irish Regt will detail a Patrol to cover the relief.

9. Completion of relief will be notified to Battn H.Q. by the code message "Sergt SMITH not here".

10. Acknowledge.

Capt & Adjt.

Dinners at 5. p.m.

Cooks to be warned to be ready at 4.30.

Operation Order No 59 by Lt-Col HE Norton
Commdg South Irish Horse (7th R. Irish)
17th Feby 1918

An inter-Coy relief will take place on the night of the 18th/19th as follows:—
"B" Coy will relieve "C" Coy
"S" " " "A" "
respectively in the Front Line.

On completion of relief the Battalion will be disposed as under:
"S" Coy in Front Line
"A" " in Support
"B" " holding Post on left of Front Line and finding its own Support
"C" Coy in Reserve.

Trench Stores will be taken over and also all information about the line, etc.

Coy Commanders will arrange between themselves all other details including the Patrol to cover the relief.

The undermentioned Officers will be attached to "B" Coy during their tour in the line:
2/Lieut Smyth
~~2/Lieut Bailey~~

Sheet 2.

Relief to be complete by 7.30 p.m. and wired to Battn. H.Q. by the code "Rum Received".

2/Lieut King will report to O.C. S. Coy by 4 p.m. to-morrow

(Sd) B. J. Start
Capt & Adjt.

SECRET   Copy No. 11

OPERATION ORDER NO. 58 BY LIEUT COL H.E. NORTON, COMMANDING

SOUTH IRISH HORSE, 7th. R. IRISH REGT. ....13/2/18.
~~~~~~

1. The South Irish Horse will relieve the 15th. Durham Light
Infantry on the night of 14th/15th in the Left Sub Section of
the Left Sector.
    "A" Coy S.I.H. will relieve "A" Coy Durham L.I.
    "B" "   "   "   "   "C" "   "   "
    "C" "   "   "   "   "B" "   "   "
    "S" "   "   "   "   "D" "   "   "

    All movement will be by Platoons at 5 minute intervals
    "A" Coy will commence to move at 5 p.m.
    1st. Platoon of "C" Coy will move at 5-20 p.m.
     "   "   " "B" "   "   "   " 5-40 p.m.
     "   "   " "S" "   "   "   " 6-15 p.m.

2. One Officer per Coy and one N.C.O. per Platoon and No.1
of Lewis Gun Teams will proceed to the Line on the night of
13th./14th. Parade at Orderly Room at 6 p.m. The Servant of
each Officer will accompany him.
    O.C. "A" Coy will detail 6 O.R. to proceed with this
Party and take over Patrol Duties.
    Rations for this Party to be made up in Sandbags and labelled

3. The following will be carefully taken over :-
    (a) Trench Stores
    (b) All Defence Schemes and Documents connected with the
        Line
    (c) Aeroplane Photographs
    (d) Work in Progress and Proposed (In writing)
    (e) Maps.
    (f) Working Parties
    Copies of (a) (d) and a list of (e) and a Sketch showing
dispositions will be forwarded to Battn H.Q. by 12 Noon 15th

4. The Guides of the Durham L.I. (4 per Coy i.e.,1 per Platoon)
will meet the Battalion at the Cross Roads V.1.c.7.5 at 6-15 p.m.
on 14th. inst.

5. All Anti-Aircraft Lewis Guns will be relieved by 12 Noon
14th. inst. Should they not be relieved by that hour they will
be withdrawn.

6. Brigade Ammunition and Bomb Store - EPEHY F.1.e.8.1.
    Brigade H.Q.   - SAULCOURT
    Battalion H.Q.   - K.25.c.8.3

7. Rations and Water etc., for "A" and "S" Coys may be brought
up to the Cookhouses in 14-WILLOWS ROAD
    The above also applies to "B" and "C" Coy and H.Q. Cookhouses
in the Railway Cutting.
    There is a Water Point in EPEHY

8. One Limber per Coy will be available - the Fore portion for
Lewis Guns and Ammunition and the Rear Portion for Officers Mess
Kit. These Limbers will precede the leading Platoon of each Coy
Lewis Guns and Magazines for same will be removed from Limber
and carried when it is no longer possible for Limber to proceed
further or keep in touch.
    One Limber, Maltese Cart and Officers Mess Cart will be at
the disposal of Battn H.Q.
    The G.S. Baggage Wagons will also be available for the removl
removal of blankets, Officers Kits etc.
    The whole of the above Transport will report to Battn H.Q.
at VILLERS FAUCON at 4 p.m.

9. Officers Kits and all surplus blankets above one per man
will be stacked as near the Cookers as possible. The blankets

Sheet 2

roller in bundles of ten and the whole under the charge of the .Q
Q/Q.M.S. who will be responsible for same.
H.Q. Officers Kit Surplus Stores and Blankets
will be stacked outside Battn H.Q. at the same hour. H.Q.
Sergeant will be responsible for the handing over of these to
the R.Q.M.S.

2/Lieut. Conway will take charge of H.Q. and establish them
at new Battn H.Q.

10. Relief will be reported to Battalion H.Q. by the Code
message "Your R.D. 58 completed"

11. Acknowledge

(Sd) B.J. Start, Capt & Adjt.

Copies to :-

Nos 1 to 4   To Coys.
No 5   To Bd H.Q.
No 6   "To 15th Durham Light Infantry
No. 7 Transport Officer
No. 8 Medical Officer
No. 9 Signalling Officer
No 10 File
No. 11 War Diary
No. 12 R.S.M.
No. 13 Lewis Gun Officer.

SECRET   Copy No 9

Operation Orders No 57 by Lieut Col H E Norton. Coy
            Commanding (South Irish Horse) 7th R. Irish Regt
            8th Feby 18.

1. The Battalion will relieve the 2nd R. Irish Regt at VILLERS
FAUCON on 9th Feby '18. Relief to be complete by 1 P.M.

2. An Advance Party consisting of 2/Lieut Conway, W.C.2.M.S.S.
Sergant Cooke and 2 Signallers from H.Q. will report to
the Town Major VILLERS FAUCON at 10 a.m. on 9.2.'18 and
take over billets etc.

3. Lewis Gun Sections for Anti-Aircraft Duty will relieve the
2nd R. Irish Regt Guns by 12 noon at the following places:—
   E 27. b. 4. 6 — one Gun
   E 27. d. 4. 9 — one Gun
The Anti-Aircraft Guns now manned by us will be
relieved by the 2nd R. Irish Regt by 12 noon.
Four Lewis Guns with Nos 1 & 2 of each gun will take over
positions on the mound at VILLERS FAUCON.
The Lewis Gun officers will arrange above and detail
sections etc.
Rations for these parties will be under Coy arrangement.

4. Battalion will parade at 10 a.m. Companies moving
off in following order at 100 yards interval.
   "A" Coy
   "C" Coy
   "S" Coy
   "B" Coy
   H.Q.

4. Blankets in excess of 1 per man will be rolled in
bundles of ten and handed into Coy. Q.M Stores by 8.30 a.m.
Transport Officer will ~~be detailed by Transport Officer~~ arrange
for the collection of these and officers kits.

6/ One limber per Coy will be detailed to report to Coys at 8.30 A.M.
Fore part to be used by Lewis Guns and Rear Part for officers
Mess Kit. Horses will be brought to convey Cookers.
Officers Mess Cart, one limber & maltese cart will report
at Battn H.Q. at 8.30 A.M.

7/ Completion of Relief will be notified to Batta H.Q. by Code
Words "Your T.T. received"

8/ Acknowledge   (Sd) B. J. Start
                                          Capt & Adjt.

No.9 War Diary

49th Brigade
16th Division.

7th BATTALION

ROYAL IRISH REGIMENT

MARCH 1918

WAR DIARY or INTELLIGENCE SUMMARY

Army Form C. 2118.

7 (S.I.H.) R. Irish Regt. Vol. 28

Place	Date	Hour	Summary of Events and Information	Remarks and references to Appendices
			7th (S.I.R.) Royal Irish Regiment — March 1918	
	11.6.P 16.P 10 to 12		Holding Line EPEHY Sector	
	13.2.17		Holding Line LEMPIRE Sector. Battn H.Q. LANCASTER HOUSE. Relieved on night 12/13 by 4th Royal Inniskilling Fusiliers.	
			The Battn moving into Brigade Reserve, manning the RONSOY Defences with 3 Coys	
			RONSOY VILLAGE	
	18/19		Relieved the 2nd Royal Irish Regt in the line, with H.Q. at BASSE BOULOGNE	
	19/20		Holding 6/10 line. S. 13 Coys in front line; A.C. Coys at RONSOY in support	
	20th		A & C Coys relieved S & B Coys in the front line; S & B Coys going in support at RONSOY	
	21st	4.30	The enemy opened a heavy bombardment mostly with gas shells - lasting about 4 hours.	
			This morning was very foggy	
		8.30	The enemy attacked and broke through A and C Coys and reached RONSOY VILLAGE before S&B Coys were aware that the attack had commenced. No news of A or C Coys got back to the rest of the Battn who were killed or taken prisoners. The enemy had practically surrounded this village before the Battn in the RONSOY line knew it, as we had broken through the Division on the right. At this time all the officers with the exception of the C.O. Adjutant had become casualties, M.O. Medical officer, details also etc. The men who had been ordered to withdraw and fought their way back to ST EMILIE where they arrived about 4 p.m. The strength there was 1 officer and about 40 other Ranks which included 5508 Sgt Moloney and 7683 Cpl Harrison. About 7 p.m. the Battn was relieved by a Battn of Gordons and moved back to VILLERS FAUCON	

Army Form C. 2118.

WAR DIARY
or
INTELLIGENCE SUMMARY.
(Erase heading not required.)

Instructions regarding War Diaries and Intelligence Summaries are contained in F.S. Regs., Part II. and the Staff Manual respectively. Title pages will be prepared in manuscript.

SHEET 2

Place	Date	Hour	Summary of Events and Information	Remarks and references to Appendices
	22nd		Enemy continued to attack during the morning. The Batt. now forming part of a composite Batt. of units of 6th Division fought their way back to THIEPVAL WOOD, where they were then formed as a company of the 49th Brigade Battalion	
	23rd		Continued rear-guard fighting back to RIVER SOMME and over, through PERONNE to BIACHES	
	24th		The Coy still forming part of the 10th Brigade Batt. took up a position SOUTH of the SOMME near MERICOURT sur SOMME	
	26th		10th Brigade Batt. moved forward to positions between CHUIGNOLLES and RIVER SOMME	
	26th		Retired to positions between CHUIGNOLLES and MERICOURT sur SOMME	
	27th		Retired through MORCOURT and LAMOTTE and took up a position to the EAST of HAMEL WOOD	
	28th		Holding line EAST OF HAMEL WOOD	

Officers joining during the month:-
Major J. Ball D.S.O. 4.3.18, Captain T.S. Snowden 24.3.18.
2nd Lieut. Wills 9.3.18, 2nd Lieut. J. Gibson D.C.M. 10.3.18, 2nd Lt. J.W. Loughlen 29.3.18, 2nd Lt. E. Woods M.M. 31.3.18
Lt. P. Beer Rejoined 30.3.18

Officers leaving during the month:-
2nd Lt. A.B. Russell to U.K. sending though to Major Cross 1.3.18, Lt.Col. J.E. Harlow to Sick leave 9.3.18
2nd Lt. R.K. Slater was to U.K.(sick) 23.3.18, 2nd Lt. T.B. Woodward to T.M.B. 10.3.18

Army Form C. 2118.

WAR DIARY
or
INTELLIGENCE SUMMARY.
(Erase heading not required.)

SHEET 3

Place	Date	Hour	Summary of Events and Information	Remarks and references to Appendices

Officers Casualties during the month:—

Business of Lieut. Major L. Colt D.S.O. 21.10.18. ?, Maj. J. D. Lewis N. 21.3.18. Capt. L. M. Ward M. 21.3.18.
 2nd Capt. R.E. Smith 21.3.18. 2nd Lt. D. R. B. Tolman M.C. 21.3.18. 2nd Lt. J. Q. Scott 21.3.18.
 Capt. R.W. Lee J. Start 21.3.18. 2nd Lt. W.B. Conrad 21.3.18. 2nd Lt. J.R. Nations 21.3.18. 2nd Lt. O.P.B. Huddley 21.3.18.

Officers missing:— 2nd Lt. F. P. Douglas (A) 21.3.18. 2nd Lt. F. O. Downs (B) 21.3.18. 2nd Lt. R.H. Lane M.M. 21.3.18.
 2nd Lt. J.W. G. Davis M.M. 21.3.18. 2nd Lt. H.A. Innes 21.3.18. 2nd Lt. H.G. Palmer 21.3.18. 2nd Lt. J. Seargeant 21.3.18.

Officers Died of Wounds:— Capt. L.E. Mackie 21.3.18
 Killed :— Lt. A.G. Depman 21.3.18.
 Wounded :— Capt. A.E. Burdge 22.3.18. Lt. E.A. Davis 21.3.18. 2nd Lt. L.C. Thornley 21.3.18.
 2nd Lt. Cotter 21.3.18. 2nd Lt. F.R. Lees 22.3.18. 2nd Lt. L. Trump 21.3.18.

" Wounded + Missing:— 2nd Lt. J.V. Jones (B) 21.3.18.

Officers sent to Hospital 2nd Lt. W.C. Purdie 9.3.18

Reinforcements received during month:—
 2nd Lt. Woods M.M. 6.3.18, 2nd Lt. J.A. Lloughlin 12.3.18

N.W. [signature]
O.C.

Lieut Col.
Comdg 2/4 Devon Regt

7(3IH) M Lan. Rgt.

Army Form C. 2118.

WAR DIARY
INTELLIGENCE SUMMARY.
(Erase heading not required.)

Vol 2   April 1918

Place	Date	Hour	Summary of Events and Information	Remarks and references to Appendices
	1/16		7th (3.I.H.) Royal Lanc. Regiment. Holding the line at HAMEL WOOD	
SAILEUX	1/16		Relieved and moved to SAILEUX en route to reorganizing area	
TOURS-EN-VIMEAU	5th 6/7/69		Moved to TOURS-EN-VIMEAU by march route. Re-organising the Battalion.	
	9		Moved to WOINCOURT by march route	
WOINCOURT	10th		Marched to EU and entrained there for ARQUES	
ARQUES	11th		Arrived at ARQUES and proceeded by march route to CAMPAGNE	
CAMPAGNE	12th		Proceeded by march route to WAVRANS	
WAVRANS	12/16th 14th		The remnants of the Battn. formed 3 Coys. of 6th and 7th Bde Composite Battn.	
			Proceeded by march route to HERBELLE	
HERBELLE	15th		Proceeded by march route to STEENBECQUE	
STEENBECQUE	15/16/8		The Battalion was made up that day by 2 H Q Linen	
"	18		1. Officer & 106 Other Ranks, all ex-cavalry men were sent to Cavalry Base for	
			retraining to cavalry units. Also 6 Officers & 50 Other Ranks of the 2nd Royal Scots Regt. also a number of N.C.O.	
			Battn. Comdgr & 3 Officers to Base Depot formed a training staff for training Conscripted Units. The 1st line transport with horses and harness	
			with the excess G.S.	
	19th		The training staff proceeded in march route to THEROUANNE	
THEROUANNE			Proceeded by march route to ILNES	

Army Form C. 2118.

WAR DIARY
or
INTELLIGENCE SUMMARY.
(Erase heading not required.)

SHEET 2.

Place	Date	Hour	Summary of Events and Information	Remarks and references to Appendices
FLNES	30/6/24		Training Staff carried out intensive training.	
	24		Proceeded by march route to LEDINGHEM.	
LEDINGHEM	26 to 29		Training staff carried out intensive training	
LEDINGHEM	30		Proceeded by march route to THÉROUANNE.	
			Officers joining during month:- Major J. Roche Kelly M.C. 12:4:18. and took over command.	
			Lt. F.J. Brenton 5.4.18.	
			Officers leaving during month:- Capt. R.O. Blewitt 18.4.18 to Cavalry Base.	

N. Kelly Major
Cmdg. Y.(S.A.) Royal Horse Gds.

7 (S.I.H) R Inish. F.

WAR DIARY
or
INTELLIGENCE SUMMARY

Army Form C. 2118.

(Erase heading not required.) Royal Irish Regt. (May 1918)

Vol 30

Place	Date	Hour	Summary of Events and Information	Remarks and references to Appendices
THEROUANNE	May 1st		Training Staff moved from THEROUANNE to PECQUET by march routes	
PECQUET	1st		700 Irish Reinforcements, Dublins and Munsters arrived for Digging Defensive Line. These were made up into companies and administered by Training Staff	
PECQUET	2nd to 14th		Work carried out every day under 1st Cav. R.E.	
do	15th		All Irish Reinforcements handed over to the 8th K.R.R. to Training Staff	
do	"		7 (S.I.H) R Irish Regt. Training Staff moved to DOHEM by march routes	
DOHEM	16th		Training Staff moved to BLENQUIN by march route	
BLENQUIN	18th		Training Staff moved to SAMER by march route	
SAMER	19th		Training Staff moved to HALINGHEM by march route, First line transport handed over to 16th Division for use of American Army	
HALINGHEM	20th		Training Staff moved to FRENCQ by march routes	
FRENCQ	21st to 31st		Commenced training 12th M/Gun Batt. and 4th Engineer Regt. U.S.A. Instruction carried out daily in Musketry, Bombing, L/Gunn, Vest. P.B.F. also training of Transport personnel	

Officers joining during month: Capt. J. Wills M.C. R. Dub. Fus. 16.5.18 as Adjutant; 2nd Lt. J. L. England, 11 Hants Regt. 12.5.18 as Lewis Gun Instructor

Army Form C. 2118.

WAR DIARY
(2.) Contd.
INTELLIGENCE SUMMARY.
(Erase heading not required.)

Place	Date	Hour	Summary of Events and Information	Remarks and references to Appendices
			Officers leaving during month. Lt. T. S. Dunston & 2nd Lt V. Hunter both of R. Inst. Regt. to Base 4.5.18. 2nd Lt J. McLoughlin & R. Hun. Fus. to Base 5.5.18.	
			Honours + Awards during month.	
			— Military Medal — 25133 Cpl. A. Claxton; 25002 Pte. P. Adams; 25136 Pte. J. Cleary.	
			Italian Decoration Bronze Medal for Military Valour 25182 Sergt. J. C. Craigie	
	Strength 31/5/18		8 Officers 51 Other Ranks.	

J. Kelly Lt. Col.
Comdg 4 (G.T.R) R. Innisk. Fus.

www.ingramcontent.com/pod-product-compliance
Lightning Source LLC
Chambersburg PA
CBHW081441160426
43193CB00013B/2348